COOKING FOR YOUR FREEZER

COOKING FOR YOUR FREEZER

Mary Berry

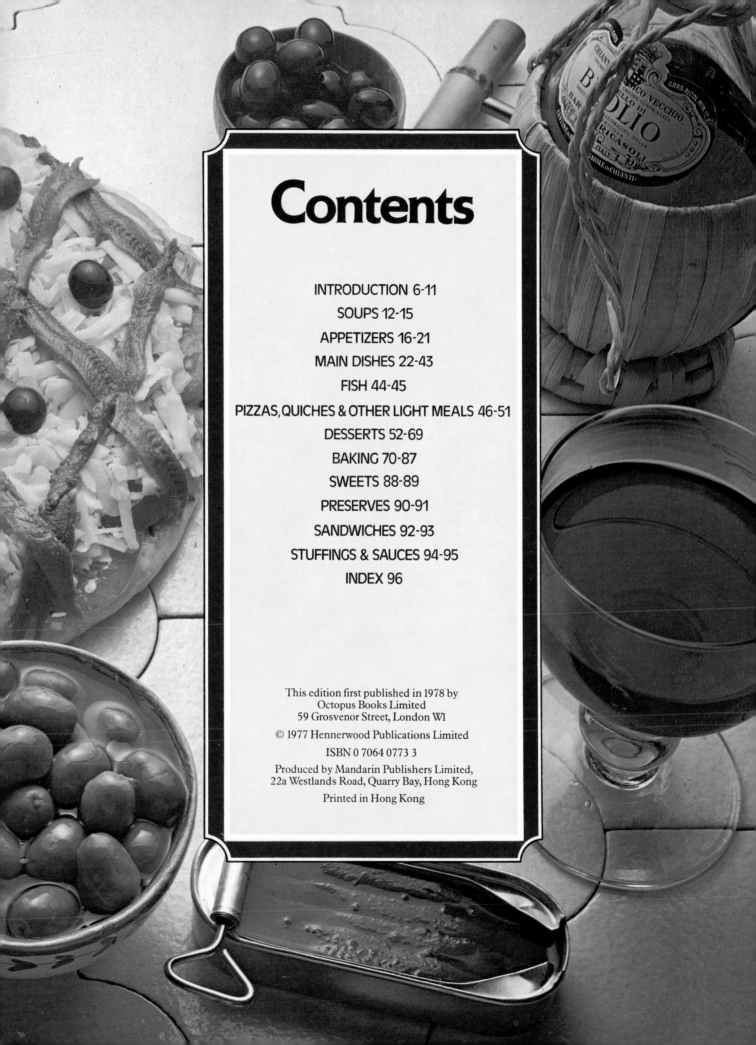

Contents

This edition first published in 1978 by
Octopus Books Limited
59 Grosvenor Street, London W1

© 1977 Hennerwood Publications Limited

ISBN 0 7064 0773 3

Produced by Mandarin Publishers Limited,
22a Westlands Road, Quarry Bay, Hong Kong

Printed in Hong Kong

Introduction

In an age which has produced all manner of labor-saving devices, the freezer is an excellent addition to household equipment. Not only is it an extra food store, but also an aid to menu planning, a stand-by in emergencies and a money-saver. But it must, of course, be used properly.

Cooking for the freezer is just as important as buying for it. The casseroles, pies, home-made soups and sauces, the cakes, pastries, toddlers' dishes which can be kept in the freezer make it a remarkable asset in the kitchen. Preparing double the quantities—half for now and half for the freezer—ensures having meals for emergencies and saves time when you are busy.

It will help the household budget too, for doubling the quantity does not mean doubling the cooking time. The amount of energy required to cook, say, one stew is the same as for cooking two.

Another advantage of the freezer is being able to cook when it is convenient and time is available. How many people throw away chicken carcasses, for example, simply because there is not time to turn them into stock. They can however be wrapped and stored in the freezer until time is available to turn them into stock.

Packaging for the freezer

Packaging is more than just a means of keeping the contents of the freezer tidy and separate. It helps to preserve the quality of the food, prevents dehydration and loss of nutritional value, stops strongly flavored foods from affecting others and inhibits bacteriological contamination between different items. For all these reasons, therefore, it pays to study the various methods of packaging carefully, decide which suits you best and buy accordingly.
Bags Plastic bags are exceptionally useful, capable of moulding themselves around awkward shapes and holding liquid if required. They come in various sizes, some with gussets and some without, separated, on a roll, colored and plain, and which you choose depends on the size of your family and how they will be used. Do buy the bags which are specially made for the freezer. They are thick enough to withstand the low temperature without splitting and if carefully washed and dried can be used again and again as a second wrap, but do not allow to contact food. Do not use bags supplied with clothes. Apart from the fact that they are not hygienic, they are also too thin to be satisfactory. *Boil-in-bags* are tough bags made to withstand being plunged straight from the freezer into boiling water. This makes them particularly valuable if you have to

go away leaving meals, mainly meat and fish in sauces, for those members of the family left at home. The dish can be prepared frozen, sealed in the bag, then heated without mess or bother. They are similar to the ones you buy containing cooked frozen meals. Other types of bag are made from aluminium foil, foil lined with plastic and paper lined with foil, and are bought with a strip seal.

Foil tins come in a great variety of shapes. Some have their own lids; others must be covered with foil. Their neat shapes make them particularly good for stacking. They are useful for complete meals, casseroles, pies and flans.

Rigid containers are usually supplied with lids and are ideal for liquids. The best are made of plastic and can be used in the refrigerator as well as in the freezer. Their tops should fit well and make an effective seal. Buy them specially for the freezer, making certain they are suitable for use at low temperatures, otherwise the plastic can become brittle and will not last long. Waxed cartons are effective and if handled carefully can be re-used if relined with a plastic bag. However they are not suitable for hot liquids and food should be cooled before being packed in these containers.

Freezer-wrap is an alternative to foil. It must be secured by means of adhesive *freezer tape*. Ordinary adhesive tape will not seal in low temperatures.

Improvised containers Don't throw away old yogurt or margarine cartons, particularly if you have a baby or toddler to feed. Enough puréed vegetables, stewed fruits, etc., for one meal, fit very nicely into a small thoroughly washed carton if it is relined with a new plastic bag. Do not use cracked containers.

Twist-ties and other seals Twist-ties, usually made from paper covered wire, are supplied with plastic bags. If you like gadgets, you can get twist-tie dispensers in which the wire comes in a continuous reel and from which you cut off the amount you need. Alternatively, there are special machines for sealing bags with adhesive freezer tape—home versions of those used by butchers. Keen freezer cooks can buy electric bag sealers but they are quite expensive.

Organizing the freezer

To be really efficient and economical, the contents of the freezer must be properly organized, so that you know where everything is and the items are used in strict rotation.

One of the best methods of storage involves grouping the same types of food together and always storing them in the same part of the freezer.

For really efficient storage it is possible to buy special stacking baskets which can be placed on the shelves of an upright freezer or stacked in the base of a chest freezer. Most chest freezers have room for three layers of baskets which helps to keep food organized in sections. Most chest freezers have one or more hanging baskets included in the purchase price. These can contain smaller articles, keeping like with like. Other baskets, some shallow, some deep, stacking or hanging, are available and enable you to make use of all the space in the freezer.

Color-Coding While not essential, this is a sensible aid to freezer planning. By giving a different color to each category of food and packing each item in an appropriately colored bag or using colored ties and labels, you can see at a glance where the meat or vegetables, the fish, fruit or pastries are.

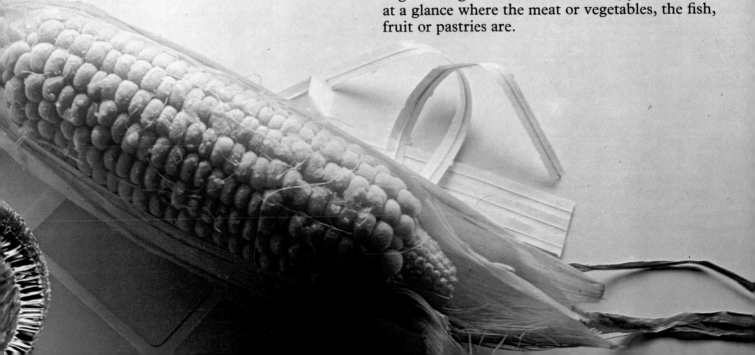

Keeping a record Always keep a list of everything the freezer contains. This prevents items from remaining in the freezer for too long and enables you to plan a menu without removing the complete contents of the freezer to see what is available. It is possible to buy special record books with ruled columns for the item, date, quantity, etc. or you can use an exercise book and rule the columns yourself. Either way, see that it is kept near the freezer, together with a pencil or pen, so that entries can be made at once, or items crossed off as food is used.

Package shapes The freezer will run more cheaply and efficiently the less free space there is between packages and if it is kept well stocked. Obviously some things like roasts are bound to be awkwardly shaped, but if possible try to freeze items into cubes or "brickets". Liquids, for example, can be poured into a plastic bag fitted inside an old sugar carton or square plastic box. When frozen, the carton "mold" can be removed. A casserole dish may be lined with foil and filled with stew to freeze. When frozen remove the dish and return it to the kitchen. Before heating, the stew can be thawed and reheated in the same dish.

Freezing food

Quality, speed and hygiene are the three watchwords of really successful freezer cooking.

Freezing won't make food *better* than it is when purchased so you should always use the best quality ingredients—young vegetables, fresh meat and fish—for best results. Speed—in cooling before freezing—limits the build up of harmful bacteria and prevents ice crystals from forming in the food, and spoiling its texture. Freezing in small quantities ensures rapid, even freezing. Hygiene is always important in the preparation of food, and food being cooked for the freezer is no exception. Very low temperatures do not destroy bacteria, they merely make them dormant and food that is contaminated before freezing will still be contaminated when thawed.

Packing food for the freezer Some dishes, such as casseroles, can be frozen in a shallow meat tin. When firm but not quite solid remove from tin, dipping the base quickly into hot water if necessary to free the contents, then cut. Wrap each block separately, seal and label and return to the freezer. Remove as much air from the package, smoothing it out with the fingers before sealing. Where possible use shallow containers rather than deep ones, so that the freezing process is quick and even.

Sealing and labeling An airtight seal is essential. Give the neck of a plastic bag a couple of twists before securing with a twist-tie or freezer tape. Labeling is equally important. Stick-on labels may be used, especially on foil, or you can write directly onto plastic bags with a permanent felt-tipped marker. Make certain the bag is dry.

The label should give as much information as possible since the contents of transparent packages look different when frozen. The quantity should be given—either by weight or the number of people it will feed. The date on which the food is frozen, or the date by which it must be used, should be shown. The dating method should be consistent and the family should be made familiar with it.

Fast freezing Most freezers, unless they are very

small, have a fast-freezing switch, which is manually operated. This over-rides the thermostat and allows the temperature within to drop below the normal running temperature of 0°F, reaching −18° to −22°F. The lower the temperature the faster the food will freeze. The temperature drops throughout the whole cabinet but the coldest places will be near the sides where the freezing elements are situated. Chest freezers usually have a fast-freeze compartment with freezing elements in the dividing wall, and it is wise to keep this free from general storage. In upright freezers, the top or bottom shelf should be used, unless your model has a special fast-freeze shelf. The reason for having special compartments is to keep the un-frozen packs away from the remainder of the contents. Even when cooled, the newly prepared food will have the effect of raising the temperature of the items with which it comes into contact and even, temporarily, of the air within the fast-freeze compartment. This is why you should not try to freeze too much at any one time—the maximum amount is 10 per cent of the freezer's loading capacity in 24 hours. Remember to operate the fast-freeze switch before you plan to do any freezing as it takes two to three hours for the temperature to be reduced. It must be left on until the food is frozen all the way through, allowing about 2 hours for each pound of meat, poultry, fish, pies and cooked meals, or

1 hour for each pound of vegetables, fruit, liquids, cakes and bread. This is very approximate: naturally a deep thick parcel takes longer to freeze than a shallow thin one.
Open freezing This is a method of freezing food before it is packed. It is particularly convenient for food which would be a nuisance if frozen firmly together, such as vegetables, cakes, rissoles, fish cakes, etc. It is essential to open freeze items which squash easily, such as the decoration on iced cakes. Open freezing may be used to make storage easier. Garden peas, for example, can be divided into the amounts needed for a meal, packed in bags and frozen. With open freezing, however, the peas will be separated and, once frozen, will flow freely and can be packed into one bag and used in small quantities when needed. For open freezing, the items are spread on a special stacking open-freeze tray or onto a baking sheet lined with foil. They are packed into containers only when frozen solid.

Freezing vegetables

Only freeze vegetables which are young and freshly picked. Start by preparing them as if for immediate use. Always wash well.

All vegetables are better if they are blanched before freezing; that is, scalded briefly in boiling water. A blanching basket is usually recommended for the purpose, but a nylon muslin wine-straining bag bought from a home brewing shop is just as effective. Using only a small quantity at a time, put the prepared vegetables into the bag or basket and lower into boiling water. Take the blanching time from the moment the water comes back to the boil. Each batch must be cooled before being packed into bags, sealed and labeled, and placed in the fast-freeze compartment for freezing. Cooling is carried out by immersing bag or basket in cold water to which you keep adding ice cubes. Alternatively, the vegetables can be put in a colander and cooled under running water. Cooling times are the same as blanching times.

Occasionally, if you have a glut of vegetables, it is possible to freeze without blanching. The results, however, should be eaten within two months as the enzymes present in the vegetables, which are inactivated by blanching, continue to be active at very low temperatures and will cause changes in color, flavor and texture.

Blanching times The following is a guide to blanching times:

Asparagus—2–4 minutes; eggplants—4 minutes; whole string beans or thickly cut string beans—2 minutes; coarsely sliced runner beans—1 minute; broad beans—2 minutes; broccoli—3–4 minutes; Brussels sprouts—3 minutes; carrots—3–5 minutes; cauliflower—3 minutes; celeriac—4 minutes; corn-on-the-cob—4–8 minutes; zucchini—1 minute; leeks—2–4 minutes; onions—2 minutes; parsnips—2 minutes; peas—1 minute; spinach—2 minutes; rutabagas—3 minutes; turnips—2 minutes. Mushrooms should be sautéed in butter, drained and cooled.

Freezing fruit

There are various ways of freezing fruit and much depends on how you intend to use it. Only freeze top quality fruit, just ripe. If over-ripe, purée first. Otherwise dry pack (freeze whole, without any additions), or stew gently, or prepare and either layer with sugar or cover with sugar syrup. Fruits such as peaches, apricots and pears, which are liable to discolor, should have ascorbic acid (Vitamin C) added to the cold syrup before freezing. The proportions: $\frac{1}{4}$ teaspoon ascorbic acid to $2\frac{1}{2}$ cups syrup.

Thawing

Whether to thaw food or not, and how long dishes should be left to thaw, are two problems which puzzle people from time to time. Generally speaking most cooked foods are best thawed just before reheating—it saves fuel too. Food can be cooked from its frozen state, provided you remember to allow a longer cooking time, with a slightly lower temperature, and do not try to speed things up by increasing the heat. Vegetables, indeed, taste better if plunged into boiling water straight from the freezer.

Meat is best thawed before being roasted, but if you must cook meat from frozen, choose a roast with a bone in, allow 45 minutes per pound for beef and lamb at 350°F; 1 hour per pound for pork at 400°F. It is advisable to have a meat thermometer to check that the inside of a roast is properly cooked. Raw poultry however *must* always be fully thawed before cooking so that it can cook quickly right through to the bone, thus ensuring the destruction of harmful bacteria which may be present. Some fruits, such as strawberries and raspberries, should not be thawed for too long as they tend to become soft and are much nicer while still slightly chilled.

Whatever you decide to thaw, it is best to allow the process to take place in the refrigerator overnight. If necessary, perhaps because you haven't given yourself enough time, food can be left to thaw at room temperature but cover well and do not allow to stand after thawing. A loaf of bread may be wrapped in foil and left to warm gently in the oven. Bread slices can be toasted from frozen.

Storage times

Cream and cream cheese containing less than 40 per cent butter fat separate when frozen. Heavy cream should be whipped for storing in the freezer.

Salad vegetables (lettuce, cucumber, etc.) will become limp and can only be frozen in the form of soups. Tomatoes may be frozen but will not afterwards be suitable for salads.

Whole eggs break in the freezer and if hard-boiled become rubbery. It is best to beat eggs for storage in the freezer.

Cooked whole boiled potatoes and spaghetti become soft in the freezer but roast potatoes and mashed potato toppings on such things as shepherd's pie and fish pies are quite successful.

Mayonnaise curdles after freezing.

Yogurt separates after freezing. Commercially frozen yogurt, however, contains a stabiliser. Plain yogurt freezes if you first add a tablespoon of honey.

Previously frozen food should not be re-frozen. Once thawed, it deteriorates more quickly than fresh food. That is to say, after a certain time its flavor and texture will begin to deteriorate although there will still be no danger to health. It can, however, be used for cooked dishes which are then frozen. If you want to serve food which is sure to be at its best, you should not exceed the storage times given in the column opposite:

Most vegetables—12 months raw mushrooms—1 month; cooked mushrooms —3 months; onions—3–6 months.
Most fruit including purées—12 months unpitted fruit—3 months; fruit pies—6 months.

Uncooked meats: lamb—6 months; pork—3 months; beef—8 months; ground meat, variety meats, tripe—3 months; bacon, vacuum-packed —5 months; smoked ham—2 months; sausages— 2 months.

Poultry etc.: chicken—12 months; duck— 6 months; giblets—2 months; game—6 months.

Fish: white—3 months; oily—2 months.

Cooked dishes: pies, casseroles, etc.—3 months.

Cakes, bread, pastry, etc.—6 months; sandwiches and biscuits—2 months; crisp bread and rolls—1 week; enriched bread, soft rolls— 4 months; breadcrumbs, croûtons—6 months; risen dough—2 weeks; unrisen dough—1 month; yeast—1 month.

Dairy produce: cream—3 months; eggs, unsalted butter—6 months; salted butter, cream with more than 35 per cent butter fat, hard cheese—3 months; cream cheese—6 weeks; Camembert, Brie cheeses freeze well—3 months.

All recipes serve four unless otherwise stated.
Cooking times given at the beginning of recipes apply only to cooking done before freezing. All instructions for cooking and serving after freezing are given at the end of recipes.

All spoon measurements are level.

Summer soup

1 bunch watercress
Outside leaves 2 heads of Boston lettuce
4 tablespoons butter
1 onion, peeled and sliced
3–4 potatoes, peeled and sliced
2½ cups chicken stock
Salt and freshly ground black pepper

Cooking Time: 30 minutes

Milk and cream are added to the soup after thawing and reheating to prevent curdling.
Wash the watercress but do not remove the stalks, wash and roughly shred the lettuce. Melt the butter in a pan and gently cook the onion and potato for 5 minutes, without browning. Add the stock and seasoning, bring to the boil, cover and simmer for 15 minutes. Add the watercress and lettuce and simmer for an additional 10 minutes, then purée through a sieve or in a blender.
To freeze: pour into a rigid container, cool, cover, label and freeze.
To cook and serve: thaw overnight in the refrigerator. Turn into a non-stick pan, then heat through, stir in 2 cups boiling milk and ⅔ cup cream. Taste and adjust seasoning, garnish each serving with a sprig of watercress.

Beet soup

1 lb cooked beets, skinned
3–4 potatoes, peeled
2 tablespoons butter
1 small onion, peeled and chopped
5 cups chicken stock
Salt and freshly ground black pepper

Cooking Time: about 50 minutes

Cut the beets and potatoes into large dice. Melt the butter in a large pan, add the onion, beets and potatoes and fry gently for about 5 minutes, stirring occasionally. Stir in the stock and seasoning and bring to the boil, then lower the heat and cover the pan. Simmer for 45 minutes, or until tender. Rub the soup through a sieve or purée in a blender.
To freeze: turn into a rigid container, cool, cover, label and freeze.
To serve: thaw overnight in the refrigerator. Turn into a saucepan and reheat gently. Taste and adjust seasoning. Serve piping hot. Stir a spoonful of heavy cream into the center of each serving if desired.

Chinese cabbage and pepper soup

2 tablespoons oil
4 tablespoons butter
½ lb green peppers, seeded, cored and diced
2 onions, peeled and chopped
½ head Chinese cabbage or celery cabbage, shredded
4 tablespoons flour
2 cups chicken stock
Salt and freshly ground black pepper

Cooking Time: 35 minutes

Heat the oil in a saucepan, then add the butter. When it has melted, add the peppers, onion and Chinese cabbage and cook gently for 5 minutes. Blend in the flour and cook for 1 minute. Gradually stir in the stock and bring to the boil. Season and simmer, covered, for 30 minutes or until the vegetables are cooked. Purée the soup in a blender or force through a sieve.
To freeze: turn into a rigid container, cool, cover, label and freeze.
To cook and serve: thaw overnight in the refrigerator. Turn the soup into a saucepan with 2 cups milk and heat through. Taste and adjust seasoning and just before serving, stir in 3 tablespoons cream.

Quick pea soup

2 tablespoons bacon fat
3 large scallions, peeled and chopped
Outside leaves of a Boston lettuce,
roughly shredded
1 lb frozen peas
4⅓ cups stock or water
Salt and freshly ground black pepper

Cooking Time: about 10 minutes

Melt the bacon fat in a pan, add the scallions and lettuce leaves and cook for 2 minutes. Add the peas, stock and seasoning, bring to the boil and simmer gently for about 5 minutes. Sieve, or purée in a blender.
To freeze: turn into a rigid container, cool, cover, label and freeze.
To serve: thaw overnight in the refrigerator. Place in a non-stick saucepan and reheat gently, taste and adjust seasoning, stir in 3 tablespoons cream and pour into bowls. Garnish with croûtons, if desired.

Iced Spanish soup

5 tomatoes, skinned and seeded
1 large onion, peeled
1 large green pepper, seeds and
pith removed
Half a cucumber
3 small cloves garlic
2 tablespoons chopped parsley
2 slices white bread without the crusts
Salt and freshly ground black pepper
2 tablespoons wine vinegar
2 tablespoons oil
A few drops Tabasco sauce
1¼ cups iced water

Make this soup when the tomatoes are at their most plentiful and cheap.
Place all the ingredients together to purée through a sieve or in a blender until smooth (place in the blender in two or three batches). Turn into a bowl and mix well.
To freeze: turn into a rigid container, cover, label and freeze.
To serve: thaw completely at room temperature, about 8 hours, stir thoroughly and spoon into serving bowls. Place an ice cube in the center of each bowl. Serve very cold, with small separate bowls of chopped cucumber, onion, tomato, green pepper, and fried bread croûtons.

Leek and artichoke soup; Iced Spanish soup

Leek and artichoke soup

1½ lb Jerusalem artichokes
2 tablespoons butter
½ lb leeks, washed and sliced
3¾ cups stock
Salt and freshly ground black pepper
Bay leaf

Cooking Time: about 50 minutes

Put the artichokes in a pan and cover with cold water, bring to the boil, cover and simmer for 15 minutes, then drain well and peel. Rinse out the pan and melt the butter in it, add the leeks and cook for 2 to 3 minutes, add the artichokes, stock, seasoning and bay leaf, cover and simmer for about 30 minutes. Remove the bay leaf and purée through a sieve or in a blender.
To freeze: turn into a rigid container, cool, cover, label and freeze.
To serve: thaw at room temperature for about 8 hours. Place in a saucepan with 1¼ cups milk and bring to the boil, stirring. Taste and adjust seasoning. Serve garnished with mint, if desired.

Vichyssoise

1½ lb leeks
4 tablespoons butter
½ lb onions, peeled and chopped
4 potatoes, peeled and diced
5 cups chicken stock
1 teaspoon salt
Freshly ground black pepper

Cooking Time: about 1 hour

Trim the tops of the leeks to within 1 inch of the white stem and cut off the roots. Slice lengthwise through the center and wash thoroughly in cold water; shred. Melt the butter in a large pan, add the onion and the leeks, cover and cook gently for about 10 minutes. Add the potatoes and cook for another 10 minutes, then stir in the stock and seasoning, cover and simmer for 30 to 40 minutes. Purée the soup in a blender, or sieve. Taste and adjust seasoning, leave to cool.
To freeze: turn into a rigid container, cover, label and freeze.
To serve: thaw at room temperature for about 8 hours or overnight in the refrigerator. Turn into a saucepan, preferably non-stick, and reheat. Remove from heat, stir in ⅔ cup cream, sprinkle with parsley and serve. For a special occasion, serve this soup cold—stir thoroughly when thawed, then stir in the cream and sprinkle with parsley, or a few snipped chives.
Serves 6

Quick pea soup; Vichyssoise

Cheese straws

1¾ cups flour
½ teaspoon salt
Pinch pepper
4 tablespoons butter
1 chicken bouillon cube
1 cup grated Cheddar cheese
½ cup grated Parmesan cheese
2 egg yolks
Cold water

Sift the flour, salt and pepper into a bowl. Add the butter, cut into small pieces, with the crumbled bouillon cube and rub in until the flour resembles breadcrumbs. Add the cheeses with the egg yolks and stir well, add enough cold water to make a firm dough.

Roll out on a floured surface to ¼ inch thickness. Trim the edges to make a neat square or rectangle then cut into straws each about ¼ inch wide and 2½ inches long. Re-roll the trimmings and cut out 6 or 8 circles about 3 inches in diameter, then cut out the centers with a 2 inch cutter to form rings.

To freeze: lay the straws and rings on a baking sheet or flat dish and open freeze. Pack in a rigid container, seal, label and return to freezer.

To cook: place on baking sheets and bake in a moderately hot oven (400°F) for 15 minutes or until golden brown. Cool on a wire rack for 10 minutes, then thread the straws through the rings.
Makes about 80

Party small ham quiches

For the pastry:
1¾ cups flour
½ teaspoon salt
4 tablespoons butter
4 tablespoons lard
2 tablespoons water

For the filling:
1 shallot, peeled and chopped
1 tablespoon butter
¼ lb ham, finely chopped
¾ cup grated Gruyère cheese
2 eggs
6 tablespoons light cream
2 teaspoons chopped chives
Salt and freshly ground black pepper

Cooking Time: 40 minutes
Oven: 375°F, then reduce to 325°F

Make the pastry in the usual way (see Leek and Ham Quiche, page 48). Roll out the dough on a floured surface and cut out 20 circles large enough to line muffin tins. Press the circles into the tins, line them with wax paper and dried beans and bake in the center of a moderately hot oven for 15 minutes. Remove paper and beans. Reduce oven temperature to warm.

Place the shallot in a small pan with the butter and cook gently for about 5 minutes. Mix shallot with the ham and divide the mixture between the pastry cases, sprinkle a little cheese in each.

Blend together the eggs, cream, chives and seasoning, spoon the mixture into the cases.

Bake in a warm oven for about 20 minutes or until the filling is set. Remove from tins.

To freeze: cool, pack in a plastic bag, seal, label and freeze.

To serve: place in a moderate oven (350°F) for 15 to 20 minutes. Serve hot.

Cheese straws; Party small ham quiches; Smoked haddock pâté

Smoked haddock pâté

1 lb smoked haddock fillet
4–6 tablespoons butter
⅔ cup heavy cream
⅔ cup light cream
3 hard-boiled eggs, finely chopped
Salt and freshly ground black pepper

Line broiler pan with foil, lay on the haddock fillet and dot with butter, broil on both sides for about 10 minutes or until the fish flakes easily. Remove the skin and any bones from the haddock and put in an electric blender with any cooking juices and the butter. Reduce to a purée and turn into a bowl. Whisk the two creams together then fold in the fish purée and hard-boiled eggs. Season well and turn into a foil dish and smooth the top.
To freeze: Cool, cover and label, then freeze.
To serve: Thaw overnight in the refrigerator and serve with hot French bread or toast.
Serves 6.

Scallops in shells

¼ lb scallops
¼ lb haddock
⅔ cup milk or dry white wine
Slice of onion
Sprig of parsley
Bay leaf
4 tablespoons butter
6 tablespoons flour
2 cups milk
½ cup grated cheese
Salt and freshly ground black pepper
Mashed potato with 1½ lb potatoes

Cooking Time: about 15 minutes

Rinse and slice the scallops. Cut the haddock into small pieces and remove any skin and bone. Place the fish in a pan with the milk or wine, onion, parsley, bay leaf, bring to the boil, simmer for 5 minutes. Drain and keep the liquid on one side. Melt the butter, add the flour and cook for a minute, stir in the fish liquid and milk and bring to the boil, stirring. Add the cheese, scallops and haddock and season well.

Divide the fish sauce between 4–6 scallop shells, or individual ovenproof dishes, and pipe the mashed potato in a border around the edge of each dish.

To freeze: open freeze, then pack in plastic bags, seal and label and return to the freezer.

To cook: take from the freezer, remove the bags, and either cook at once in a hot oven (425°F) for about 1 hour, or thaw in the refrigerator for about 8 hours and then reheat in a hot oven for about 15 minutes.

Salmon and egg mousse

⅓ oz gelatin
6 tablespoons water
⅔ cup condensed consommé
6 oz salmon
3 hard-boiled eggs
⅔ cup mayonnaise
⅔ cup heavy cream, whipped
Salt and freshly ground black pepper
1 tablespoon chopped parsley

An ideal way of using up the last of the fresh salmon left over from a dinner party.

Put the gelatin in a bowl with the water, leave to soak for 5 minutes. Stand over a bowl of simmering water and stir until gelatin is dissolved. Add to undiluted consommé. Flake the salmon and remove any pieces of skin and bones. Finely chop the eggs, place in a bowl with the salmon, mayonnaise, cream and three-quarters of the consommé mixture and mix together well, taste and season. Pour into a quart dish and leave until set. Add the parsley to the remaining consommé and pour over the mousse, leave until set.

To freeze: cover dish with foil, label and freeze.

To serve: thaw overnight in the refrigerator. Decorate with slices of hard-boiled egg.

Kipper mousse

10 oz kipper fillets
Butter
1¼ cups heavy cream
2 tablespoons lemon juice
Pinch cayenne

Place the kipper fillets, skin side up, in a baking dish, dot with butter and heat through under the broiler. Reserve the cooking butter.

Remove all the dark skin and bones from the kipper fillets and pass through a sieve, or place them in a blender, with the cream, the reserved butter and the lemon juice. Blend until smooth, add cayenne to taste.

Turn into 6 individual ramekin dishes.

To freeze: cover, label and freeze.

To serve: thaw overnight in the refrigerator. Garnish each dish with slices of stuffed olive and serve with hot toast.

Serves 6

Scallops in shells; Kipper mousse; Salmon and egg mousse; Taramasalata

Taramasalata

2 slices crustless white bread
¼ cup cold milk
6 oz jar smoked cod's roe
1 clove garlic, crushed
9 tablespoons oil
2 tablespoons lemon juice
Salt and freshly ground black pepper

Soak the bread in the milk and squeeze dry. Blend all the ingredients together, taste and adjust seasoning.
To freeze: turn into a small foil dish, cover, label and freeze.
To serve: thaw overnight in the refrigerator and serve with lemon wedges and hot toast or French bread.

Avocado and onion dip

2 avocados
Scant $\frac{1}{2}$ cup cream cheese
3 tablespoons lemon juice
$\frac{1}{4}$ small onion, peeled and very
finely chopped
Freshly ground black pepper

Cut the avocados in half and remove the pits, scoop out the flesh, put it in a bowl and mash well with a fork. Add the remaining ingredients and stir until well blended.
To freeze: place in a small rigid container, cover, label and freeze.
To serve: thaw at room temperature for 4 to 5 hours, turn into a bowl and serve with potato chips, stalks of celery or carrot or small sausages.

Garlic bread

2 cloves garlic
$\frac{1}{2}$ teaspoon salt
Freshly ground black pepper
$\frac{1}{4}$ lb (1 stick) butter
1 teaspoon chopped dried thyme and basil
1 teaspoon chopped parsley
1 loaf French bread

Crush the garlic with the salt to a smooth paste and put in a bowl with the pepper, butter and herbs. Cream well. Cut the loaf along in 1 inch slices to within $\frac{1}{2}$ inch of the bottom. Spread the slices on each side with the garlic butter and press together again. Wrap in foil.
To freeze: label and freeze.
To cook: thaw at room temperature for 3 to 4 hours, then heat in a moderately hot oven (400°F) for 12 to 15 minutes, still in foil, until hot and crisp.

Grapefruit and melon refresher

1 small ripe melon
1 grapefruit, peeled and segmented
2 tablespoons lime juice
$\frac{1}{4}$ cup sugar

Halve the melon and remove the seeds. Peel the melon halves, cut the flesh into cubes and place in a rigid container with the grapefruit segments, lime juice and sugar. Leave to stand for 1 hour.
To freeze: cover, label and freeze.
To serve: thaw in the refrigerator overnight. Serve in 4 wine glasses.

Canadian style pâté

1 lb salt belly of pork
$\frac{1}{2}$ lb lean pork
$\frac{1}{4}$ lb pigs' liver
1 onion, peeled
2 cloves garlic, crushed
A little salt
Freshly ground black pepper
1 tablespoon chopped parsley
3 tablespoons sherry
5 slices Canadian style bacon

Cooking Time: $1\frac{1}{2}$ to 2 hours
Oven: 325°F

Remove any rind and bones from the belly of pork and cut into small pieces, grind into a bowl with the lean pork, liver and onion. Add the garlic, seasoning, parsley and sherry, mix well together. Line the base and sides of an ovenproof dish with bacon, spread in the pork mixture, cover with a piece of foil, stand in a dish of water and bake in a warm oven for $1\frac{1}{2}$ to 2 hours.
To freeze: cool completely, then turn out and wrap in a double thickness of foil, put in a plastic bag, seal, label and freeze.
To serve: thaw in the refrigerator overnight, or for 6 hours at room temperature. Serve with hot toast or French bread.

Grapefruit and melon refresher; Avocado and onion dip; Canadian style pâté; Garlic bread

Basic Scotch mince; Savory mince pies; Cottage pie; Curry pies

Savory mince pies

1 portion Basic Scotch mince (see right)
Shortcrust pastry made with 2⅔ cups flour
(see page 48)

Place the mince in a bowl and make sure it is cold. Roll out two-thirds of the pastry and cut into six 5 inch circles and line six 4 inch foil dishes. Roll out the remaining pastry and cut out six 4 inch circles for lids. Divide the mince between the pies, dampen the edges and cover with the lids. Seal the edges firmly with the prongs of a fork or the tip of a metal spatula. Decorate with pastry trimmings.

To freeze: wrap the pies individually in a double layer of foil, seal, label and freeze.

To cook: unwrap, glaze with milk or beaten egg, make a small slit in the center of each pie and bake in a hot oven (425°F), for 25 to 30 minutes until golden brown.

Makes 6 individual pies

Cottage pie

1 portion Basic Scotch mince (see below)
½ lb carrots, peeled and grated
1 tablespoon chopped parsley
Salt and freshly ground black pepper
1 lb potatoes, boiled
Knob of butter
A little milk

Combine the mince with the carrot and parsley, taste and adjust seasoning. Turn into a pie dish. Sieve or mash the potatoes, add the butter and milk, season to taste, spread over the top of the meat and mark with a fork. Decorate with extra potato, if liked.
To freeze: open freeze, then wrap in foil, label and return to freezer.
To cook and serve: remove wrapping and cook from frozen in a moderately hot oven (400°F) for 1½ to 1¾ hours. Garnish with finely chopped parsley.

Basic Scotch mince

2 tablespoons drippings
(melted beef fat)
1 lb onions, peeled and chopped
2 tablespoons tomato paste
4 teaspoons salt
Freshly ground black pepper
⅓ cup plus 2 teaspoons flour
4⅓ cups water
2 beef bouillon cubes
4 lb ground beef

Cooking Time: about 1 hour

Cook the beef at one go and pack in 4 portions. A meat roasting tin is ideal as this way, you can freeze until it is almost solid, then turn it out like a gelatin mold, leave until just (but only just) thawed enough to cut into quarters, pack in plastic bags, label and return at once to the freezer.
Heat the drippings in a large pan, add the onion, stir and fry over a low heat until soft and lightly colored. Stir in the tomato paste, seasoning and flour and cook for 2 minutes. Add the water and bouillon cubes with the ground beef and bring to the boil, stirring. Cook gently, stirring occasionally, until cooked through, about 30 to 45 minutes in a shallow pan and an hour for a deeper pan.
Remove from heat and cool quickly.
To freeze: as suggested above or pack in 4 rigid containers, or make into recipes and then freeze.
To serve: thaw and use as required.

Curry pies

Make as Savory Mince Pies, but when putting the mince in a bowl, stir in 1 teaspoon (or to taste) curry powder, 1 tablespoon chutney and about ¼ cup golden raisins. Freeze, and bake as Savory Mince Pies.
Makes 6 individual pies.

Italian meat balls

¾ lb sausage meat
2 tablespoons oil
¾ lb onions, peeled and sliced
1 clove garlic, crushed
4 stalks celery, scrubbed and sliced
1 green pepper, seeded and sliced
3 tablespoons tomato paste
1¼ cups cider or stock
¼ lb mushrooms, cleaned and sliced
2 teaspoons sugar
Salt and freshly ground black pepper
½ lb noodles
1 cup grated Cheddar cheese

Cooking Time: about 30 minutes

Divide the sausage meat into small pieces and roll into 24 small balls on a lightly floured surface. Heat the oil in a large pan and add the meat balls, onion and garlic and fry until brown. Add the celery, pepper, tomato paste, cider or stock and mushrooms and bring to the boil, add the sugar and seasoning. Simmer for 20 minutes. Cook the noodles as directed on the package, drain well and stir into the sauce with the cheese. Taste and adjust seasoning. Turn into a rigid container.
To freeze: cool, cover, label and freeze.
To serve: thaw at room temperature for 8 hours, then turn into a casserole, cover and heat through in a moderate oven (350°F) for 1½ hours, stirring occasionally.

Beef Oxford

2 lb stewing beef
4 tablespoons flour
4 tablespoons drippings (melted beef fat)
Salt and freshly ground black pepper
$\frac{1}{2}$ lb onions, peeled and sliced
2 cloves garlic, crushed
$\frac{1}{4}$ lb mushrooms, cleaned and sliced
1 green pepper, seeded and sliced
2 tablespoons apricot jam
$1\frac{1}{4}$ cups red wine
$1\frac{1}{4}$ cups beef stock

Cooking Time: 2–2$\frac{1}{2}$ hours

Cut the meat into neat pieces, put in a plastic bag with the flour and toss until well coated. Melt the drippings in a pan and fry the meat quickly to brown. Add all the remaining ingredients, including any flour left in the bag, bring to the boil, cover and simmer for 2 to 2$\frac{1}{2}$ hours or until the meat is tender, stirring occasionally.
To freeze: turn into a rigid container, cool, cover, label and freeze.
To serve: thaw overnight in the refrigerator, place in a saucepan and reheat gently, stirring until piping hot.
Serves 6

Italian meat balls; Beef Oxford

Meat balls in sweet and sour sauce

¾ lb ground beef
1 cup fresh white breadcrumbs
1 egg
Salt and freshly ground black pepper
2 tablespoons oil
1 onion, peeled and finely chopped
2 carrots, peeled and cut into long strips
1 leek, washed and finely sliced
2 stalks celery, scrubbed and finely sliced
4 teaspoons cornstarch
2 teaspoons sugar
1¼ cups water
2 tablespoons tomato ketchup
1 tablespoon vinegar
1 tablespoon soy sauce

Cooking Time: 40 minutes

Place the ground beef, breadcrumbs, egg and seasoning together in a bowl and mix well. Turn onto a floured board and shape into 16 meat balls. Heat the oil in a pan and fry the meat balls until brown all over, lift onto a plate. Add the onion, carrot, leek and celery to the pan and fry slowly. Place the cornstarch and sugar in a bowl and gradually stir in the water, add the ketchup, vinegar and soy sauce, pour into the pan and bring to the boil, stirring. Return the meat balls to the pan, cover with a lid and simmer for 30 minutes.
To freeze: turn into a rigid container, cool, cover, label and freeze.
To serve: thaw at room temperature for 4 to 5 hours, turn into a saucepan and heat through gently. Serve if liked with ribbon noodles.

Spaghetti sauce

1 lb lean ground beef
A little drippings (melted beef fat)
2 slices bacon, chopped
2 tablespoons flour
3 stalks celery, scrubbed and chopped
½ lb onions, peeled and chopped
1¼ cups water
1 clove garlic, crushed
1 beef bouillon cube
Salt and freshly ground black pepper
¼ teaspoon dried oregano, parsley and basil
3 tablespoons tomato paste
Few Spanish stuffed green olives, sliced

Cooking Time: 1¾ hours

Place the beef and drippings in a pan with the bacon and cook slowly until the fat has run out, then brown, turning frequently. Add the flour and blend well. Stir in all the other ingredients, except the olives, bring to the boil, cover and simmer for about 1 hour or until tender. Add the olives and taste and adjust seasoning.
To freeze: turn into a rigid container, cool, cover, label and freeze.
To serve: thaw overnight in the refrigerator or at room temperature for about 6 hours, turn into a saucepan and reheat gently. Serve with spaghetti.

European lasagne; Meat balls in sweet and sour sauce; Spaghetti sauce

European lasagne

$3\frac{1}{2}$ tablespoons butter
4 tablespoons flour
$2\frac{1}{2}$ cups milk
$\frac{1}{4}$ teaspoon prepared mustard
A little ground nutmeg
$\frac{1}{4}$ teaspoon salt
5 oz lasagne
1 cup grated Cheddar cheese
$\frac{1}{2}$ cup grated Gruyère cheese
2 tablespoons grated Parmesan cheese
1 quantity Spaghetti sauce (see opposite)

To make the white sauce, melt the butter in a pan, add the flour and cook for 1 minute. Add the milk and bring to the boil, stirring, add the mustard, nutmeg and salt. This sauce will have a thin pouring consistency. Take a 9 inch square foil dish, and put in a layer of white sauce, then cheese, meat sauce and dried lasagne. Repeat and finish with a final layer of white sauce and cheese. Do not overlap the lasagne, break the pieces if necessary to fit the dish.
To freeze: leave to become quite cold, cover, label and freeze.
To cook: thaw for 24 hours in the refrigerator, or 12 hours at room temperature. Remove the lid and cook in a moderately hot oven (375°F) for about $\frac{3}{4}$ to 1 hour, until golden brown.
Note: the sauces are more runny than usual to allow the raw pasta to cook and absorb the liquid.
Serves 5 to 6 portions

Beef curry

2 lb stewing beef
4 tablespoons flour
1½ teaspoons salt
1 large onion, peeled and chopped
4 tablespoons margarine
3 teaspoons curry powder
1 tablespoon paprika
1¼ cups beef stock
2 dried red chillies
1 tablespoon mango chutney
1 teaspoon Worcestershire sauce
1 lb can pineapple chunks
2 bay leaves

Cooking Time: 1¾ hours

Cut the beef into ¾ inch cubes and toss in the flour and salt.
Put the onion in a pan with the margarine and fry until soft, stir in the curry powder and paprika, fry for 2 minutes then add the beef, stir well and cook for 5 minutes.
Add the remaining ingredients to the pan, including the pineapple syrup. Cover and cook gently for 1½ hours or until tender. Remove the bay leaves and chillies and taste and adjust the seasoning.
To freeze: cool, turn into a rigid container, cover, label and freeze.
To serve: thaw overnight in the refrigerator or for 6 to 8 hours at room temperature. Turn into a casserole and heat through in a moderate oven (350°F) for 45 minutes. Serve with boiled rice.

Steak and kidney pies

½ lb stewing beef
½ lb ox, veal or lamb kidney
4 tablespoons flour
2 tablespoons drippings (melted beef fat)
1 large onion, peeled and chopped
1¼ cups beef stock
Salt and freshly ground black pepper
¼ lb mushrooms, cleaned and sliced
Shortcrust pastry made with 2⅔ cups flour (see page 48)

Cooking Time: 1½ hours

Cut the meat and kidney into ½ inch cubes and toss in the flour. Heat the drippings in a pan, add the onion and fry for 2 to 3 minutes. Add the meat and fry until browned. Stir in the stock and seasoning and bring to the boil, partially cover and simmer for 1¼ hours. Add the mushrooms and cook for another 15 minutes. Taste and adjust seasoning and leave to cool.
Roll out two-thirds of the pastry and cut into six 5½ inch circles and line six 4 inch foil dishes. Roll out the remaining pastry and cut six 4 inch circles for lids. Divide the filling between the pies. Dampen the edges and cover with the lids. Seal the edges firmly with the prongs of a fork.
To freeze: cool and wrap each pie individually in a double layer of foil, label and freeze.
To serve: unwrap, glaze with milk or beaten egg, make a small slit in the center of each pie. If liked, put into ovenproof dishes, and bake in a hot oven (425°F) for 25 to 30 minutes until golden brown.
Makes 6 individual pies

Beef curry; Hot spiced crêpes; Steak and kidney pies

Hot spiced crêpes

A little drippings (melted beef fat)
¾ lb ground beef
3 tablespoons flour
¼ teaspoon Tabasco sauce
¼ teaspoon ground ginger
Salt
8 oz can tomatoes
1 clove garlic, crushed
1 teaspoon Worcestershire sauce
1 teaspoon wine vinegar
8 crêpes (see page 55)

Cheese sauce:
2 tablespoons butter
3 tablespoons flour
1¼ cups milk
½ cup grated Cheddar cheese
1 teaspoon prepared mustard
Salt and freshly ground black pepper

Cooking Time: 1 hour

Melt the drippings in a pan and add the beef, fry, stirring, for 3 to 4 minutes until any fat runs out. Add the flour and cook for 1 minute, add Tabasco sauce, ginger, salt, tomatoes, garlic, Worcestershire sauce and vinegar, bring to the boil, cover, reduce the heat and simmer for 45 minutes until cooked. Taste and adjust seasoning, leave to cool.

Divide the filling between the crêpes and roll up. Lay in a single layer in a foil dish.

To make the cheese sauce, melt the butter in a pan and stir in the flour, cook for 1 minute, add the milk and bring to the boil, stirring. Simmer until thickened then stir in the cheese, mustard and seasoning. Pour over the crêpes and leave to cool.

To freeze: cover, label and freeze.

To serve: thaw in the refrigerator overnight, remove the lid, sprinkle with grated Cheddar cheese and bake in a moderately hot oven (400°F) for 30 minutes, until golden brown. Serve with a salad.

Moussaka

4 large eggplants
Salt
7 tablespoons oil
1 lb ground lamb
½ lb onions, peeled and chopped
3 tablespoons flour
1 clove garlic, crushed
16 oz can tomatoes
Pinch each dried thyme, basil
and marjoram
2 tablespoons chopped parsley
Freshly ground black pepper
1¼ cups cheese sauce (see page 29)
½ cup grated Cheddar cheese

Cooking Time: 25 minutes

Slice the eggplants, sprinkle with salt and leave for 30 minutes. Drain and dry on paper towels. Fry the slices in 6 tablespoons oil until brown on both sides. Remove from the pan and drain. Put the remaining oil in the pan with the lamb and brown. Add the onion and cook for 10 minutes. Blend in the flour, garlic, tomatoes and herbs, bring to the boil and taste and adjust seasoning. Arrange the eggplant slices and lamb mixture in layers in a buttered shallow ovenproof dish. Pour over the cheese sauce and sprinkle with the extra cheese. Cool.
To freeze: open freeze, remove from the dish, put in a plastic bag, seal, label and return to freezer.
To serve: remove plastic bag, return the moussaka to the dish and reheat in a moderately hot oven (400°F) for 1 hour.

Creamed pork

1 lb pork fillet
3 tablespoons butter
6 tablespoons flour
2½ cups stock
½ lb small carrots, peeled
Salt and freshly ground black pepper
¼ lb mushrooms, cleaned

Cooking Time: 1 hour

Cut the pork into ½ inch slices. Melt the butter in a pan, add the pork and fry quickly for 3 to 4 minutes to seal the juices, remove the pork and put on one side. Stir the flour into the butter in the pan and cook for 1 minute. Add the stock and bring to the boil, stirring, return the pork to the pan. Cut the carrots in quarters lengthwise, add to the pan with the seasoning, cover and simmer for 45 minutes. Add the mushrooms and cook for another 15 minutes.
To freeze: cool, turn into a rigid container, cover, freeze.
To serve: thaw overnight in the refrigerator, turn into a saucepan and reheat gently, stirring occasionally, bring to the boil. Just before serving remove pan from the heat and stir in ⅔ cup light cream, turn into a dish.

Lamb steaks in piquant sauce

4 tablespoons butter
1 large onion, peeled and chopped
1 clove garlic, crushed
2 tablespoons flour
16 oz can tomatoes
1 tablespoon tomato paste
1 tablespoon brown sugar
¼ teaspoon paprika
3 tablespoons vinegar
Salt and freshly ground black pepper
4 lamb leg steaks

Cooking Time: ¾ to 1 hour

Place the butter in a small pan and fry the onion and garlic for 5 minutes until golden brown. Stir in the flour and cook for 1 minute. Add the can of tomatoes, tomato paste, sugar, paprika and vinegar and cook together for 3 to 4 minutes. Taste and adjust seasoning. Lay the lamb in a shallow ovenproof dish and pour over the sauce. Cover and bake for ¾ to 1 hour until the lamb is tender.
To freeze: cool quickly, cover, label and freeze.
To serve: thaw at room temperature for 6 hours then reheat in a moderate oven (350°F) for 45 minutes.

Lamb steaks in piquant sauce; Spiced pork rolls; Creamed pork; Moussaka

Spiced pork rolls

$\frac{1}{2}$ lb pork sausage meat
Finely grated rind of $\frac{1}{2}$ lemon
Pinch each dried thyme, parsley, bay leaf,
basil and marjoram
4 pork escalopes
2 tablespoons oil
2 tablespoons butter
1 onion, peeled and chopped
1 tablespoon paprika
1 tablespoon flour
1$\frac{1}{4}$ cups stock
5 tablespoons sherry
1 teaspoon tomato paste
Salt and freshly ground black pepper
$\frac{1}{2}$ lb mushrooms, cleaned

Cooking Time: about 45 minutes.

Mix the sausage meat with the lemon rind and herbs, divide the
mixture between the escalopes, spread flat then roll up and secure
with two pieces of string or wooden cocktail sticks. Fry quickly in
the oil and butter until just beginning to brown, then remove from
the pan.
Add the onion and paprika to the pan and cook for 3 minutes, stir
in the flour, remove the pan from the heat and stir in the stock,
sherry and tomato paste. Return to the heat and bring to the boil,
stirring, simmer until the sauce has thickened.
Add the pork rolls to the pan with seasoning, cover and simmer
for 45 minutes or until tender. Stir in the mushrooms and cook for
2 to 3 minutes.
To freeze: remove the string or cocktail sticks from the pork rolls,
then turn into a rigid container, cool, cover, label and freeze.
To serve: thaw overnight in the refrigerator. Place in a saucepan
and reheat gently until piping hot, remove the pan from the heat
and stir in $\frac{2}{3}$ cup sour cream just before serving.

Frugal Irish stew

Frugal Irish stew

Large breast of lamb, on the bone
1 lb onions, peeled and sliced
2 lb potatoes, peeled and sliced
Salt and freshly ground black pepper
$\frac{1}{2}$ lb carrots, peeled and sliced
1 teaspoon chopped fresh thyme or
$\frac{1}{2}$ teaspoon dried
Water

Cooking Time: 2 hours
Oven: 325°F

Cut the lamb into neat serving pieces and trim off any excess fat.
Put half the onion into a 2 quart casserole, add half the potato and then the meat, seasoning each layer well. Cover with the carrots, then add the remaining onion and finish with a layer of potato. Add the thyme and enough water to come half way up the casserole. Cover and cook in a warm oven for 1 hour, then remove the lid and cook for another hour.
To freeze: cool quickly, cover, label and freeze.
To serve: thaw completely overnight in the refrigerator, then reheat in a modern oven (350°F) for about 1$\frac{1}{2}$ hours, until hot through.

Lamb with Spanish rice stuffing

Lamb with Spanish rice stuffing

1 can or package Spanish rice
3 lb boned shoulder of lamb
A little marjoram
2 tablespoons drippings (melted beef fat)
1 tablespoon flour
1¼ cups stock
1 tablespoon tomato paste
Salt and freshly ground black pepper

Cook the rice according to the directions on the package. Remove from the heat and leave to cool.

To freeze: place the meat in a plastic bag, seal, label and freeze. Place the rice in a container, label and freeze.

To cook: thaw meat and rice overnight in the refrigerator. Put the rice into the cavity in the shoulder, then put the meat back into shape and secure with skewers. Place the meat in a roasting pan and sprinkle it with marjoram, add the drippings and roast until the meat is tender (about 1½ to 2 hours in a moderate oven—350°F). Remove and place on a serving dish.

Pour off all but 1 tablespoon of the drippings and stir in the flour, cook, stirring, for 1 minute over a low heat. Add the stock and tomato paste and bring to the boil, add the seasoning and taste and adjust, simmer for 2 minutes then serve with the meat. Garnish with a few sprigs of watercress.

Serves 8

33

Kidneys in sherry sauce

4 tablespoons butter
1 onion, peeled and chopped
8 lambs' kidneys
3 tablespoons flour
$1\frac{1}{4}$ cups stock
6 tablespoons sherry
1 tablespoon redcurrant jelly
$\frac{1}{2}$ teaspoon salt
Freshly ground black pepper

Cooking Time: 15 minutes

Melt the butter and fry the onion until golden brown. Wash, skin and core the kidneys and cut each into 3 pieces. Add to the pan and fry for 5 minutes, stirring. Add the flour, stir in the stock, sherry and redcurrant jelly with the seasoning, bring to the boil and simmer for 5 minutes.

To freeze: turn into a rigid container, cool, cover, label and freeze.

To serve: place in a casserole and reheat in a moderate oven (350°F) for 40 minutes, or until piping hot.

Shoulder of lamb with raisin and apricot stuffing

1 onion, peeled and chopped
1 tablespoon butter
8 oz can apricots
1 cup fresh white breadcrumbs
2 tablespoons finely chopped parsley
$\frac{1}{2}$ cup raisins
$\frac{1}{2}$ teaspoon salt
Freshly ground black pepper
1 egg, beaten
Small boned shoulder of lamb
Drippings (melted beef fat)

Fry the onion in the butter in a small pan until golden brown. Drain the apricots (reserve the juice to use in the gravy) and roughly chop. Mix the onion with the apricots, breadcrumbs, parsley, raisins and seasoning and bind together with the beaten egg.

To freeze: put the stuffing into the cavity in the meat and sew up or secure with skewers. Place the meat in a plastic bag, seal, label and freeze.

To serve: thaw meat and stuffing overnight in the refrigerator. Put in a roasting pan with the drippings and roast in a moderate oven (350°F) for $1\frac{1}{2}$ to 2 hours, or until tender. Serve with gravy. Use this recipe within one month.

Braised ox heart

3 tablespoons drippings (melted beef fat)
1 lb ox, beef or veal heart, washed, trimmed and sliced
3 tablespoons flour
$2\frac{1}{2}$ cups water
1 beef bouillon cube
2 onions, peeled and chopped
2 carrots, peeled and chopped
2 stalks celery, scrubbed and chopped
Salt and freshly ground black pepper
1 bay leaf
A little gravy browning

Cooking Time: 2–3 hours

Heat the drippings in a large pan and fry the heart quickly on both sides to brown, remove from the pan. Stir the flour into the fat remaining in the pan and cook for 1 minute, then stir in the water and bring to the boil, add the bouillon cube and stir until dissolved. Return the heart to the pan with the vegetables, seasoning, bay leaf and gravy browning, cover and simmer until tender (up to 3 hours). Taste and adjust seasoning and remove the bay leaf.

To freeze: turn into a rigid container, cool, cover, label and freeze.

To serve: thaw overnight in the refrigerator. Reheat, preferably in a non-stick pan, for about 10 minutes.

Kidneys in sherry sauce; Pork and corn pies; Braised ox heart; Shoulder of lamb with raisin and apricot stuffing

Pork and corn pies

$\frac{3}{4}$ lb lean pork
4 tablespoons seasoned flour
2 tablespoons drippings (melted beef fat)
1 large onion, peeled and finely chopped
1$\frac{1}{4}$ cups chicken stock
Salt and freshly ground black pepper
1 cup corn

For the pastry:
2$\frac{2}{3}$ cups flour
6 tablespoons lard
6 tablespoons margarine
Cold water to mix
Milk to glaze

Cooking Time: 1$\frac{1}{2}$ hours

Trim the pork and cut into $\frac{1}{2}$ inch cubes. Toss in the flour. Heat the drippings in a pan, add the onion and fry for 2 to 3 minutes. Add the meat and fry until browned. Stir in the stock and seasoning and bring to the boil, partially cover and simmer for 1$\frac{1}{4}$ hours or until tender; stir in the corn and cook for 2 minutes. Taste and adjust seasoning, leave to become quite cold. Place in a large strong pie dish. Make the pastry in the usual way (see page 48).
Roll out two-thirds of the pastry, cut out three ovals to line three small pie dishes. Roll out the remaining pastry and cut out three ovals for lids. Divide the filling between the pies. Dampen the edges with water and cover with the lids. Seal the edges firmly.
To freeze: wrap each pie in a double layer of foil, label and freeze.
To serve: unwrap, thaw overnight in the refrigerator or for 4 to 5 hours at room temperature. Make a slit in the center of each pie, glaze with milk and bake in a hot oven (425°F) for 40 minutes, or until the pastry is golden brown.
Makes 3 two-portion pies.

Coq au vin

Coq au vin

1 chicken, quartered, or 4 pieces
2 tablespoons butter
1 tablespoon oil
¼ lb chunk bacon
1 large onion, peeled and sliced
2 stalks celery, scrubbed and chopped
1 clove garlic, crushed
3 tablespoons flour
1¼ cups red wine
1¼ cups stock
Salt and freshly ground black pepper
¼ lb mushrooms, cleaned and sliced

Cooking Time: 1¼ hours

Remove the skin from the chicken pieces, melt the butter in a pan with the oil and fry the chicken until brown, remove and put in a flameproof casserole. Trim rind from bacon, cut in strips, add to the pan with the onion and celery and fry until soft, transfer to the casserole. Add the garlic and flour to the fat remaining in the pan and cook until brown, stir in the wine and stock and bring to the boil, season to taste, pour over the chicken, cover and cook for 45 minutes. Add the mushrooms to the casserole and cook for a further 15 minutes or until the chicken is tender. Taste and adjust seasoning.
To freeze: turn into a rigid container, cool, cover, label and freeze.
To serve: thaw overnight in the refrigerator, turn into a casserole, cover and reheat in a moderate oven (350°F) for 45–50 minutes. If liked, put into a heated serving dish.

Country pheasant casserole

Country pheasant casserole

2 tablespoons oil
2 tablespoons butter
2 stewing pheasants
½ inch slice bacon, rinded and diced
4 tablespoons flour
1¼ cups red wine
1¼ cups chicken stock
2 tablespoons apple jelly
1 tablespoon Worcestershire sauce
¼ teaspoon fresh thyme
1 teaspoon salt
Plenty of freshly ground black pepper
Little gravy browning
16 small white onions, peeled

Cooking Time: 2¼ hours

Heat oil and butter in a large shallow pan, brown the pheasants over a medium heat, turning as each side becomes golden brown. Lift out onto a plate. Quickly fry the bacon, to extract the fat, in the butter remaining in the pan, lift out and place with the pheasant. Add flour to the pan and cook until a pale golden brown. Slowly add the wine and stock, bring to the boil and allow to thicken. Add the remaining ingredients, except the onions, return the pheasants to the pan, bring to the boil, cover and simmer for 1½ hours, add the onions and cook for another ½ hour. Test birds for tenderness by piercing the leg with a fine skewer, do not overcook. Lift out the pheasants carefully and carve the meat. Taste and adjust seasoning and, if necessary, add more gravy browning to give a good color.
To freeze: cool quickly, arrange the slices of pheasant in a rigid container and spoon over the sauce. Cover, label and freeze.
To serve: thaw overnight in the refrigerator, carefully place in a casserole, making sure that the slices of meat are in the bottom of the dish, and reheat in a moderate oven (350°F). Arrange the pheasant slices and onions in a heated serving dish and pour over the sauce. Garnish with sprigs of parsley.

MAIN DISHES
Chicken risotto

6 oz flavored rice
½ lb cooked chopped chicken
¼ lb cooked chopped frankfurter or
sausage

Cook the rice as directed on the package, remove from the heat and stir in the chicken and frankfurter, mix well. Allow to cool.
To freeze: Place in a rigid container, cover, label and freeze.
To serve: thaw overnight in the refrigerator. Stir in ¼ lb frozen peas, turn into a well buttered ovenproof dish, cover and heat through in a moderate oven (350°F) for 45 minutes.

Chicken paprika

3¼ lb chicken
1¼ cups dry cider
Salt and freshly ground black pepper
2 tablespoons butter
1 onion, peeled and chopped
3 teaspoons paprika
3 tablespoons flour
1 lb tomatoes, skinned and seeded
1 clove garlic
1 bay leaf

Cooking Time: about 2 hours
Oven: 350°F

Put the chicken with the giblets in a small roasting pan or casserole, add the cider and seasoning, cover with a piece of foil or a lid and cook in a moderate oven for 1½ hours, or until tender. Lift the chicken out to cool, strain off the stock in the pan and skim off the fat.
Melt the butter in a small pan, add the onion and cook for 5 minutes until soft, stir in the paprika and cook for 3 minutes. Add the flour and stir in the chicken stock with the tomatoes, garlic and bay leaf, simmer without a lid for 15 minutes, remove the bay leaf and taste and adjust the seasoning.
To freeze: carve the chicken into portions, lay in a rigid container and spoon over the sauce (if liked the sauce may be strained). Cool, cover, label and freeze.
To serve: thaw overnight in the refrigerator, turn into an oven-proof dish, cover and reheat in a moderate oven (350°F) for ¾ to 1 hour. Stir in a little sour cream or yogurt just before serving.

Norfolk turkey casserole

4 fresh turkey drum sticks
4 tablespoons butter
1 package mushroom soup mix
2 cups water
¼ lb mushrooms, cleaned and sliced
¼ teaspoon dried thyme

Cooking Time: 55 minutes
Oven: 350°F

Remove the skin from the drum sticks. Melt the butter in a pan and fry the turkey until golden brown, remove and place in a casserole. Stir the soup mix into the butter remaining in the pan, add the water and bring to the boil, stirring, add the mushrooms and thyme and pour over the drum sticks, cover and cook in a moderate oven for 45 minutes or until tender.
To freeze: cool quickly, turn into a rigid container, cover, label and freeze.
To serve: thaw overnight in the refrigerator, turn into a casserole and reheat in a moderate oven (350°F) for 40 minutes.

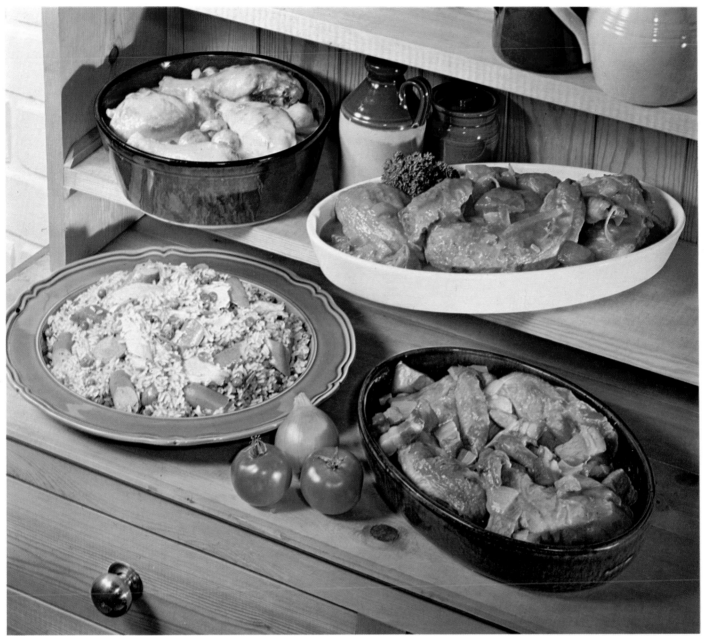

Chicken risotto; Norfolk turkey casserole; Chicken paprika; Italian country chicken

Italian country chicken

1 chicken, quartered, or 4 pieces
2 tablespoons butter
$\frac{1}{4}$ lb chunk bacon, diced
1 onion, peeled and chopped
1 clove garlic, crushed
3 tablespoons flour
$\frac{2}{3}$ cup red Italian wine
$\frac{2}{3}$ cup chicken stock
Salt and freshly ground black pepper
$\frac{1}{4}$ teaspoon dried thyme

Cooking Time: $1\frac{1}{4}$ hours
Oven: 325°F

Remove the skin from the chicken. Melt the butter in a pan and fry the chicken until brown, remove and place in a large casserole. Add the bacon to the fat remaining in the pan with the onion and garlic and fry until it is brown and the onion is soft. Stir in the flour and cook for 2 minutes. Add the wine, stock, seasoning and thyme. Bring to the boil and pour over the chicken pieces. Cover and cook in a warm oven for 1 hour, or until the chicken is tender. Taste and adjust seasoning, cool.
To freeze: turn into a rigid container, cover, label and freeze.
To serve: thaw overnight in the refrigerator, turn into a casserole, cover and reheat in a moderate oven (350°F) for 45 to 50 minutes.

Chicken in cider sauce with mushrooms

3¼ lb chicken
1¼ cups dry cider
2 onions, peeled and chopped
Salt and freshly ground black pepper
Milk
4 tablespoons butter
6 tablespoons flour
½ lb mushrooms, cleaned and quartered

Cooking Time: 1 hour 40 minutes
Oven: 350°F

Put the chicken and giblets in a small roasting pan or casserole. Add the cider, onion and seasoning. Cover with a piece of foil or a lid and cook in a moderate oven for 1½ hours or until tender. Lift the chicken out to cool and strain off the remaining stock in the pan, skim off the fat and make up to 3 cups with milk. Remove the chicken meat from the carcass, and cut it into good sized pieces. Melt the butter in a pan, add the flour, cook and stir in the stock and milk, bring to the boil, stirring, and allow to thicken. Add the mushrooms and cook for 5 minutes. Taste and adjust seasoning, stir in the chicken, turn into a rigid container and leave to cool.
To freeze: cover, label and freeze.
To serve: thaw overnight in the refrigerator, turn into a casserole and put in a moderate oven (350°F) for 45 minutes or until piping hot, turn into a serving dish, sprinkle with a little finely chopped parsley.

Chicken in cider sauce with mushrooms

Calpe chicken

¼ lb prunes
4 tablespoons butter
1 chicken, quartered, or 4 pieces
4 slices bacon, chopped
1 onion, peeled and chopped
1 carrot, peeled and sliced
3 stalks celery, scrubbed and sliced
4 tablespoons flour
⅔ cup red wine
2 cups chicken stock
Finely grated rind of ½ lemon
Salt and freshly ground black pepper

Cooking Time: 1¼ hours
Oven: 350°F

Soak the prunes overnight and then remove the pits. Melt the butter in a pan and brown the chicken on both sides, remove and place in a casserole. Add the bacon, onion, carrot and celery to the pan and fry for 3 to 4 minutes. Stir in the flour and cook for a minute. Add the remaining ingredients and bring to the boil, simmer for 1 minute to allow to thicken. Pour over the chicken, cover the casserole and cook in a moderate oven for about 1 hour or until the chicken is tender.

To freeze: turn into a rigid container, cool, cover, label and freeze.

To serve: thaw overnight in the refrigerator, or for 5 to 6 hours at room temperature, place in a casserole and reheat in a moderately hot oven (375°F) for ¾ to 1 hour.

Calpe chicken

Chicken with olives

2 tablespoons butter
1 chicken, quartered, or 4 pieces
$\frac{1}{4}$ lb chunk bacon
12 pearl onions, peeled
3 tablespoons flour
$\frac{2}{3}$ cup dry cider
$\frac{2}{3}$ cup water or chicken stock
Salt and freshly ground black pepper

Cooking Time: 1$\frac{1}{4}$ hours
Oven: 350°F

Melt the butter in a frying pan and fry the chicken until golden brown all over, remove and place in a casserole. Cut the bacon in strips, add to the frying pan with the onions and fry until brown, transfer to the casserole. Stir the flour into the butter remaining in the pan and cook for 2 minutes, add the cider and water or stock and bring to the boil, stirring, season to taste, pour over the chicken and cook in a moderate oven for 1 hour, or until tender.
To freeze: cool, turn into a large foil dish or rigid container, cover, label and freeze.
To serve: thaw overnight in the refrigerator, turn into a casserole and reheat in a moderately hot oven (375°F) for 45 minutes. Stir in 12 stuffed green olives, taste, adjust seasoning. Put onto a heated serving dish and sprinkle with chopped parsley.

Simple Devon chicken pie; Braised squabs

Chicken with olives

Simple Devon chicken pie

$\frac{1}{2}$ lb cooked chicken
$\frac{1}{2}$ lb cooked bacon or ham
$\frac{1}{4}$ lb frozen mixed vegetables, blanched
$11\frac{1}{2}$ oz can condensed mushroom soup
Shortcrust, puff or other pastry to top

Cut the chicken and ham into small even-sized pieces and place in a bowl with the vegetables and soup, mix together well. Turn into a pie dish. Roll out the pastry and use to cover the top of the pie, cut any trimmings into leaves and use as decoration.

To freeze: open freeze to prevent the decoration from being crushed. Put into a plastic bag, seal, label and freeze.

To cook: remove from the bag, thaw overnight in the refrigerator, brush the top with milk and make two small slits in the center. Bake in a moderately hot oven (400°F) for about 30 minutes or until the pastry is golden brown.

Braised squabs

2 squabs, split
4 tablespoons drippings (melted beef fat)
$\frac{1}{2}$ lb onions, peeled and sliced
4 tablespoons flour
$2\frac{1}{2}$ cups stock
3 tablespoons tomato ketchup
$\frac{1}{2}$ teaspoon fresh or $\frac{1}{4}$ teaspoon
dried marjoram
A few drops Worcestershire sauce
Salt and freshly ground black pepper

Cooking Time: 50 minutes to 1 hour

Wipe the squabs. Melt the drippings in a large pan, add the squabs and fry quickly to brown, remove and put on one side, add the onion and fry for 5 to 10 minutes until golden brown. Stir in the flour and cook for 2 minutes, add the stock and bring to the boil, stirring until thickened, add the remaining ingredients and return squabs to the pan, cover and simmer gently for 40 to 50 minutes, or until tender.

To freeze: turn into a rigid container, cool, cover, label and freeze.

To serve: thaw overnight in the refrigerator, place in a casserole, cover and reheat in a moderate oven (350°F) for $\frac{3}{4}$ to 1 hour. Serve with red cabbage (see page 48).

43

Smoked haddock crêpe rolls

7½ oz smoked haddock fillets
(finnan haddie)
Milk
2 tablespoons margarine
3 tablespoons flour
Finely grated rind of ½ lemon
Freshly ground black pepper
8 crêpes (see page 55)

Cooking Time: about 15 minutes

Drain off the liquid and make up to 1½ cups with milk. Skin and flake the fish and remove any bones. Melt the margarine in a small pan and add the flour, cook for one minute, stir in the fish liquid, bring to boil, simmer for 2 minutes to thicken. Add the haddock, lemon rind and pepper, taste and adjust seasoning. Divide the filling between the crêpes, fold in the sides and roll up.
To freeze: wrap in a double layer of foil, seal, label and freeze.
To serve: unwrap, thaw at room temperature for 4 to 5 hours. Melt 4–6 tablespoons butter in a frying pan and fry the crêpe rolls over a moderate heat until golden brown all over and hot through. Serve with a green vegetable.

Salmon fish cakes; Family fish pie

Smoked haddock crêpe rolls

Salmon fish cakes

8 oz can pink salmon
¾ lb freshly boiled and mashed potatoes
1 tablespoon finely chopped parsley
Salt and freshly ground black pepper
2 eggs, beaten
Browned breadcrumbs

Drain the salmon, flake the fish and remove any black skin and bones.
Place in a bowl with the potato, parsley, seasoning and one beaten egg. Mix well and shape into a roll, cut into 8 even-sized slices. Coat the fish cakes in the other beaten egg and then toss them in the breadcrumbs.
To freeze: open freeze, then pack in a rigid container, cover, label and return to the freezer.
To cook and serve: thaw at room temperature for 3 to 4 hours, then fry in hot oil for 4 to 5 minutes on each side until golden brown, drain on paper towels. Serve with a mixed salad.

Family fish pie

1 lb cod
1¼ cups shelled peas
2 cups milk
3 tablespoons butter
4 tablespoons flour
3 hard-boiled eggs
2 tablespoons mayonnaise
Salt and freshly ground black pepper
1½ lb potatoes, peeled
Milk and butter

Cooking Time: about 12 minutes

Skin and wash the cod, put in a pan with the peas and milk and simmer gently for 10 minutes, or until the fish can be flaked with a fork. Tip into a bowl and set on one side. Rinse out the pan and then melt the butter. Remove from the heat and stir in the flour, add the milk strained from the fish, return to the heat and bring to the boil. Remove any bones from the fish and add to the sauce with the peas, chopped hard-boiled eggs, mayonnaise and seasoning. Turn into a foil dish, leave to cool.
Boil the potatoes, drain, mash with milk and butter, taste and adjust seasoning. Spread or pipe a border round the edge of the dish.
To freeze: cool, cover, label and freeze.
To serve: thaw overnight in the refrigerator, then remove lid and reheat in a hot oven (425°F) for 30 to 40 minutes. Garnish with sprigs of parsley and sliced tomato.

Pizza

1½ 20 oz packages frozen white dough
A little oil

A yeast dough takes time to make, but the new frozen doughs are quick and easy to use, can be made in a quarter of the time and offer an ideal base for delicious toppings.

It is a good idea to make at least two pizzas at one go—more if you can. If you like the toppings, but find the bases a bit too much of a good thing, simply make them thinner.

Pizzas are usually round, but if every inch of your freezer space is valuable, oblong pizzas can be stacked into block shapes, which take up less room. Make them in a small jelly roll tin and cut to the size you want. Of course, there is no rule about size—make one big family pizza, or a lot of individual-sized ones. Experiment and find what suits you best. Do the same with flavors—you can always add to these by sprinkling at the last minute with a generous amount of grated cheese, or a few chopped herbs.

Let dough thaw and rise, following the directions on the package. Knead lightly until smooth then divide into 4 equal portions. Roll each piece out into a circle 8 inches in diameter and brush each with oil.

Topping 1:
3 slices salami
¼ cup tomato chutney
¼ teaspoon dried basil and oregano
2 large tomatoes, sliced

Topping 1:
Arrange the slices of salami on a dough circle, put the chutney and herbs in a bowl and mix well, spread over the salami. Arrange the tomato slices on the chutney to cover completely.

Topping 2:
¼ cup canned chicken spread
¼ cup canned deviled ham
8 oz can peeled tomatoes, drained and roughly chopped
1 tablespoon oil
1 onion, peeled and chopped
Freshly ground black pepper
6 stuffed green olives, sliced

Topping 2:
Spread a dough circle with the chicken and ham spreads. Place the onion and oil in a pan and cook for 5 minutes, stir in the tomatoes with the pepper and olives, mix well, cool and spread on the dough.

Topping 3:
16 oz can tomatoes, drained and roughly chopped
¼ teaspoon oregano
Salt and freshly ground black pepper
3 oz Swiss cheese
Anchovy fillets

Topping 3:
Mix the tomatoes with the oregano and seasoning, spread over the third dough circle. Cover with slices of cheese and arrange a lattice of anchovy fillets on top.

Topping 4:
2 tablespoons butter
4 slices bacon, chopped
4 mushrooms, cleaned and sliced
½ cup grated Cheddar cheese

Topping 4:
Melt the butter in a small pan, add the bacon and mushrooms and cook together for 5 minutes, drain and arrange on the last piece of dough, cover with grated cheese.

Leave all the pizzas to prove in a warm place for 15 minutes.
To freeze: open freeze until firm, then wrap in a double thickness of foil, label and return to the freezer.
To cook: unwrap, place on a lightly oiled baking tray and bake in oven (425°F) 25–30 minutes.

Pizzas: Topping 1; Topping 2; Topping3; Topping 4

Red cabbage

1 small red cabbage
¾ lb cooking apples, peeled, cored
and sliced
⅔ cup water
3 tablespoons sugar
1 teaspoon salt
3 cloves
5 tablespoons vinegar
4 tablespoons butter
1 tablespoon redcurrant jelly

Cooking Time: 45 minutes

Finely shred the cabbage, removing the hard stalk, and place with the apples and water in a pan. Add sugar, salt and cloves, cover and simmer until tender, about 45 minutes. Remove the cloves, add the vinegar, butter and redcurrant jelly and stir until the butter has melted. Taste and adjust seasoning.
To freeze: turn into a rigid container, cool, cover, label and freeze.
To serve: thaw overnight in the refrigerator, put in a non-stick pan and reheat gently, stirring.

Leek and ham quiche

For the pastry:
¾ cup flour
2 tablespoons margarine
2 tablespoons lard
1 tablespoon cold water

For the filling:
2 tablespoons butter
1 leek, washed and finely sliced
¼ lb cooked ham, chopped
Salt and freshly ground black pepper
1 egg
⅔ cup light cream

Cooking Time: 40–45 minutes
Oven: 425°F

Sift the flour into a bowl, add the fats cut in small pieces and rub in with the fingertips until the mixture resembles fine breadcrumbs, add water and mix to a firm dough. Roll out and line a 7 inch flan ring on a baking sheet. Chill in the refrigerator for 10 minutes. Fill with wax paper and dried beans and bake blind in a hot oven for 15 minutes. Remove from oven and take out the beans and paper. Meanwhile melt the butter in a small pan, add the leek and cook slowly until soft but not brown, then drain and put in the quiche case with the ham. Blend the seasoning, egg and cream together and pour into the quiche. Reduce the oven temperature and bake for 25 to 30 minutes or until the filling is set.
To freeze: cool, put in a plastic bag, seal, label and freeze.
To serve: remove from bag and thaw in the refrigerator overnight, then heat through in a moderate oven (350°F) for 25 minutes.

Onion and anchovy quiche

1 lb onions, peeled and finely sliced
2 tablespoons butter
2 tablespoons oil
1 clove garlic, crushed
Pastry made with ¾ cup flour (see above)
1 large egg
¼ cup heavy cream
Salt and freshly ground black pepper
2½ oz can anchovies

Cooking Time: about 1½ hours
Oven: 400°F

Put the onion in a pan with the butter, oil and garlic, cover and cook very slowly with the lid on until soft and golden; this may take up to one hour. Make the pastry, roll out, line a 7 inch flan ring on a baking sheet and refrigerate to rest. Remove the onion from the heat and leave to cool slightly. Beat the egg with the cream and seasoning, stir into the onion and put into the quiche case. Arrange a lattice of anchovy fillets on top of the quiche and bake in a moderately hot oven for about 30 minutes or until set.
To freeze: cool, put in a plastic bag, seal, label and freeze.
To serve: thaw in the refrigerator for several hours, then heat in a moderate oven (350°F) for 25 minutes.

Red cabbage; Stuffed eggplants; Onion and anchovy quiche; Leek and ham quiche

Stuffed eggplants

2 onions, peeled and chopped
1 clove garlic, crushed (optional)
¾ lb ground beef
4 tablespoons flour
1¼ cups water
1 teaspoon Worcestershire sauce
1 beef bouillon cube
Salt and freshly ground black pepper
2 large eggplants
1¼ cups cheese sauce (see page 29)

Cooking Time: 35 minutes

Put the onion and garlic with the ground beef in a pan and fry gently for 5 minutes, stirring frequently. Stir in the flour and water, Worcestershire sauce and add the crumbled bouillon cube and seasoning. Cover and simmer slowly for 30 minutes or until tender, taste and adjust seasoning. Cool. Halve the eggplants lengthwise and scoop out the centers, cook in boiling water for 5 minutes, drain well and place in a large foil dish. Fill with the beef mixture and spoon over the cheese sauce.
To freeze: leave to become quite cold, cover, label and freeze.
To serve: thaw at room temperature for 6 hours, then cook in a moderate oven (350°F) for 40 minutes or until hot through.

Cabbage and onion sauté

2 lb white cabbage
1–2 teaspoons salt
4 tablespoons butter
1 onion, peeled and chopped
Freshly ground black pepper

Cooking Time: about 7 minutes

Shred the cabbage fairly finely and remove all the hard white stalk, sprinkle with salt and leave to stand for 10 minutes in a bowl of cold water. Drain off the water, but do not rinse off the salt. Melt 2 tablespoons butter in a large saucepan, add the cabbage and cook until just tender, but still crisp, shaking the pan frequently to prevent sticking. Turn into a bowl. Melt the remaining butter in the pan and fry the onion until golden brown, stir into the cabbage and season with plenty of pepper. Cool.
To freeze: turn into a rigid container, cover, label and freeze.
To serve: thaw at room temperature for 5 to 6 hours, turn into a saucepan and reheat gently, stirring continuously.

Spinach and cheese quiche

For the pastry:
1¼ cups flour
3 tablespoons margarine
3 tablespoons lard
Water to mix

For the filling:
10 oz package frozen chopped spinach
1 egg
⅔ cup light cream
Salt and freshly ground black pepper
¾ cup grated Cheddar cheese

Cooking Time: 40–45 minutes
Oven: 425°F

Sift the flour into a bowl, rub in the margarine and lard until the mixture resembles fine breadcrumbs, add sufficient cold water to make a firm dough. Roll out and line an 8 inch plain flan ring on a baking sheet. Chill in the refrigerator for 10 minutes. Line with wax paper, fill with dried beans and bake blind in a hot oven for 15 minutes.
Remove from oven, take out beans and paper. Cook the spinach as directed on the package, drain very thoroughly and spread over the bottom of the quiche. Blend the egg, cream and seasonings together and pour into the quiche case. Sprinkle with the cheese. Reduce the oven temperature and bake the quiche for about 30 minutes or until the filling is set.
To freeze: cool, put in a plastic bag, seal, freeze.
To serve: thaw in the refrigerator overnight, then heat through in a moderate oven (350°F) for 25 minutes.

Asparagus quiche

Pastry made with ¾ cup flour
(see page 48)
10½ oz can asparagus tips, drained
1 egg
⅔ cup light cream
Salt and freshly ground black pepper

Cooking Time: about 45 minutes
Oven: 425°F, then reduce to 350°F

Roll out the pastry and use to line a 7 inch flan ring on a baking sheet. Chill in the refrigerator for 10 minutes. Line with wax paper, fill with dried beans and bake blind for 15 minutes in a hot oven. Remove from the oven and take out the beans and paper. Put the asparagus tips in the bottom of the quiche case. Blend the egg, cream and seasoning together and pour into the quiche. Reduce the oven temperature and bake for 25 to 30 minutes until the filling is set.
To freeze: cool, put in a plastic bag, seal, label and freeze.
To serve: thaw in the refrigerator overnight, then heat through in a moderate oven (350°F) for 25 minutes.

Celery and ham mornay; Cabbage and onion sauté; Asparagus quiche; Spinach and cheese quiche

Celery and ham mornay

1 lb 3 oz can celery hearts, drained
4 slices ham
1¼ cups cheese sauce (see page 29)
½ cup grated Cheddar cheese

Wrap each piece of celery in a slice of ham. Lay in an ovenproof dish, pour over the cheese sauce. Cool.
To freeze: cover with a piece of foil, seal, label and freeze.
To cook: thaw at room temperature for 5 to 6 hours, sprinkle with cheese and cook in a moderately hot oven (400°F) for 30 minutes or until golden brown.

Lattice mince pie

1⅓ cups flour
4 tablespoons butter
4 tablespoons lard
Pinch of salt
1 egg yolk
1 tablespoon sugar
2 teaspoons water
1 lb freezer mincemeat (see page 91)
Milk to glaze

Cooking Time: 25 minutes
Oven: 400°F

Sift the flour into a bowl, add the fats cut in small pieces, with the pinch of salt, and rub into the flour with the fingertips until the mixture resembles fine breadcrumbs. Mix the egg yolk, sugar and water together, add to the dry ingredients and bind them together. Roll out the pastry and line an 8 inch pie plate. Trim the edges. Spread the mincemeat over the pastry. Roll out the pastry trimmings and cut into 6 strips about ½ inch wide and long enough to go across the top of the pie. Twist each strip once or twice and lay them loosely over the mincemeat, three each way to make a lattice. Dampen edges and press firmly to the pastry. Brush the pastry with a little milk and bake in a moderately hot oven for 25 minutes, or until a pale golden brown, cool.
To freeze: cover with a plastic bag, seal, label and freeze.
To serve: thaw at room temperature for 4 hours then reheat in a moderately hot oven (375°F) for 20 minutes, or serve cold.

Lattice mince pie; Little mince pies

Little mince pies

3½ cups self-rising flour
¼ lb (1 stick) butter
¼ lb hard margarine
4 tablespoons lard
1 egg, separated
Milk
1½ lb freezer mincemeat (see page 91)
A little sugar

Cooking Time: 20 minutes
Oven: 400°F

Sift the flour into a bowl. Add the butter, margarine and lard cut in small pieces, then rub the fats into the flour until the mixture resembles fine breadcrumbs. Add the egg yolk with enough milk to make a firm dough. Knead until blended then chill the dough in the refrigerator for 20 minutes. Roll out half the dough thinly. Cut out about 35 circles 2¾ inches in diameter and use to line muffin tins. Fill with the mincemeat. Roll out the remaining dough and cut out 35 circles 2¼ inches in diameter for the lids. Wet the edges of the dough circles in the tin and press the lids on gently to seal. Lightly beat the egg white and brush over the tops of the pies, dust with a little sugar. Bake in a moderately hot oven for 20 minutes, or until the pastry is crisp and golden brown. Leave to cool in the tins.

To freeze: open freeze in the tins, then remove from tins and pack in plastic bags, seal and label.

To serve: replace in the tins and reheat in a moderately hot oven (400°F) for 25 minutes.

Makes about 35 mince pies

Fresh mincemeat crêpes; Rich orange crêpes; Prune and apple pie; Apricot and almond tart

Prune and apple pie

½–¾ cup prunes, soaked
1½ lb cooking apples, peeled, cored and
sliced (about 4 cups)
⅔ cup brown sugar
4 tablespoons butter
1 teaspoon ground cinnamon
Double batch Pastry (see page 48)
Milk to glaze

Cooking Time: about 15 minutes

Remove the pits from the prunes. Place the prunes and apples in a pan with the sugar, butter and cinnamon. Cook gently until the apples are just tender, stirring occasionally, leave to cool.

Make up the pastry and use half to line an 8 inch enamel or foil plate, spread in the filling, moisten the edges with water and roll out the remaining pastry to cover, press edges well together and flute.

To freeze: open freeze, then cover with a lid of foil, label and return to the freezer.

To serve: remove the foil lid, make two small slits in the top, brush with a little milk and bake in a hot oven (425°F) for 30 to 40 minutes, or until golden brown. Serve with whipped cream or ice cream.

Apricot and almond tart

Pastry made with ¾ cup flour
(see page 48)
16 oz can apricots
Rounded cup flour, sifted
¼ cup ground almonds
6 tablespoons butter
¼ cup sugar

Cooking time: 45 minutes
Oven: 400°F, then reduce to 325°F

Roll out the pastry and line a 7 inch fluted flan ring. Drain the apricots and arrange half over the base of the tart. Mix the flour with the almonds and rub in the butter, stir in the sugar. Cover the apricots with a layer of this mixture. Place the rest of the apricots on top and cover with the remaining almond mixture, pressing down firmly. Bake in a moderately hot oven for 15 minutes, then reduce the oven temperature and cook for another 30 minutes, or until a pale golden brown.
To freeze: cool, wrap in foil, label and freeze.
To serve: thaw at room temperature for 5 to 6 hours, mix a pinch of cinnamon with a little sugar and sprinkle over the tart, serve with plenty of whipped cream.

Rich orange crêpes

¾ cup flour
¼ teaspoon salt
1 egg
1 teaspoon oil
1¼ cups milk
12 tablespoons (1½ sticks) unsalted butter
Finely grated rind of one orange
2–3 tablespoons orange juice
1¾ cups sifted confectioners' sugar

Sift the flour and salt into a bowl. Blend in the egg with the oil and milk. Heat very little oil in an 8 inch pan. Drop 2 tablespoons of the mixture into the pan and tilt and rotate to spread out the batter. Cook for 1 minute, then turn over and cook the other side for 1 minute. Turn out and make seven more crêpes.
Cream the butter with the orange rind and beat in as much orange juice as possible and the confectioners' sugar.
Divide the filling between the crêpes and spread over each, then fold in four.
To freeze: wrap in a double thickness of foil, seal, label and freeze.
To cook and serve: thaw at room temperature for 4 hours. Heat a little bit of butter in a frying pan, add the crêpes and fry gently for 3 to 4 minutes on each side. Turn onto a serving dish and sprinkle with a little confectioners' sugar. Serve at once.

Fresh mincemeat crêpes

1 lb cooking apples, peeled, cored and sliced (about 3 cups)
⅔ cup brown sugar
4 tablespoons butter
¼ teaspoon ground allspice
1¼ cups mixed dried fruit (golden raisins, dark raisins, currants and candied peel)
1 tablespoon lemon juice
A little finely grated lemon rind
8 crêpes (see above)

Cooking Time: 20 minutes

Place the apples in a pan with the sugar, butter and spice and simmer gently, stirring occasionally, for 20 minutes or until tender. Stir in the dried fruit, lemon juice and rind and leave to cool. Divide the filling between the crêpes and roll up.
To freeze: wrap in a double thickness of foil, seal, label and freeze.
To cook and serve: unwrap and thaw at room temperature for 4 hours. Fry the crêpe rolls in about 6 tablespoons butter over a moderate heat until they are golden brown. Serve with plenty of whipped cream.

Orange sherbet

¾ cup sugar
2 cups water
6 fl oz can frozen orange juice, thawed
2 egg whites

Dissolve the sugar in the water, bring to the boil and boil, uncovered, for 10 minutes. Turn the frozen orange juice into a bowl and pour on the syrup. Leave to get cold then pour into an ice-cube tray and freeze to a mushy consistency. Whisk the egg whites until thick and foamy but not dry. Fold into the orange mixture and return to the freezer until firm.

To freeze: cover, label and return to freezer.

To serve: leave to soften slightly in the refrigerator for about 5 minutes then serve spooned into glasses.

Raspberry sherbet

1 lb raspberries
¾ cup sugar
2 egg whites

Purée the raspberries and measure the amount of water needed to make the purée up to 2½ cups—do not mix the purée and water together. Dissolve the sugar in the water and bring to the boil, boil uncovered for 10 minutes, stir into the raspberry purée and leave to cool, then pour into an ice-cube tray and freeze until it has a mushy consistency. Whisk the egg whites until thick and foamy, but not dry, and fold into the purée, return to the freezer until firm.

To freeze: cover, label and return to freezer.

To serve: leave to soften slightly in the refrigerator for about 5 minutes then spoon into glasses.

Red fruit salad

½ lb rhubarb, cut in ¾ inch lengths
½ lb blackcurrants
1 cup sugar
6 tablespoons water
½ lb small strawberries, hulled
½ lb raspberries

Put the rhubarb in a saucepan with the blackcurrants. Add the sugar and water and bring to the boil, simmering until barely tender, stirring; this will take only a few minutes. Add the strawberries and raspberries and cook for another minute.

To freeze: turn into a rigid container, cool, cover, label and freeze.

To serve: thaw at room temperature for 8 hours, or overnight in the refrigerator. Stir in a little brandy to taste. Turn into a serving dish and serve with whipped cream.

Red fruit salad; Raspberry sherbet; Orange sherbet

Blackcurrant sherbet

2 lb blackcurrants
¾ cup sugar
3¾ cups water
2 tablespoons lemon juice
3 tablespoons rum

Cook the blackcurrants with the sugar and water. Add the lemon juice and purée through a strainer or in a blender. Turn into a shallow container and freeze until mushy. Take out and whisk until light and fluffy and add the rum. Return to the freezer and freeze until firm.
To freeze: cover, label and return to freezer.
To serve: leave to soften slightly in the refrigerator for 5 minutes, then serve spooned into glasses.

Lemon cream ice

1 cup sugar
8 egg yolks
¼ cup lemon juice
1¼ cups heavy cream

This is a very good way of using up egg yolks if you have been making meringues.
Put the sugar on an ovenproof plate and heat through in the oven or under the broiler. Put the yolks in a large bowl, pour on the hot sugar and whisk at once until thick and light. Put the lemon juice and cream in a bowl and whisk until the cream forms soft peaks, fold into the egg mixture, turn into a rigid plastic container.
To freeze: cover, label and freeze.
To serve: leave to stand at room temperature for 5 minutes then serve—give small portions as the ice cream is very rich.
Serves 6 to 8

Blackcurrant sherbet; Lemon cream ice

Strawberry ice cream

½ lb strawberries, hulled
¼ cup sugar
2 eggs
¼ cup superfine sugar
1 small can evaporated milk, well chilled

Place the strawberries in a pan with the granulated sugar and cook gently until soft, about 5 minutes. Purée and leave to become quite cold. Separate the eggs. Place the yolks in a small bowl and blend with a fork; put the whites in a large bowl and whisk until stiff, then whisk in the superfine sugar a spoon at a time. Slowly whisk the egg yolks into the whites. Whisk the evaporated milk in a bowl until thick and fold into the egg mixture with the strawberry purée. Turn into a quart dish and leave to freeze for at least 4 hours or until set.
To freeze: cover, label and return to freezer.
To serve: leave to stand at room temperature for about 5 minutes then serve in spoonfuls in glasses.
Note: this is a good way of using frozen strawberries.

Caramel ice cream

1¼ cups fresh wholewheat breadcrumbs
⅓ cup brown sugar
4 eggs, separated
½ cup superfine sugar
1¼ cups heavy cream

Place the breadcrumbs and brown sugar on an ovenproof or foil plate and toast under a hot broiler until golden brown and caramelized, stirring occasionally. This will take 5 to 8 minutes. Leave to become quite cold.
Whisk the egg yolks in a small bowl until well blended. In another larger bowl, whisk the egg whites until stiff then whisk in the superfine sugar a teaspoon at a time. Whisk the cream until it forms soft peaks, then fold into the meringue mixture with the egg yolks and breadcrumbs. Turn into a rigid container.
To freeze: cover, label and freeze.
To serve: thaw at room temperature for 5 minutes, then serve in scoops with cookies.
Serves 6 to 8

Strawberry ice cream; Caramel ice cream

Redcurrant and raspberry mousse

½ cup sugar
1¼ cups water
½ lb redcurrants
½ lb raspberries
⅓ oz gelatin
1 tablespoon hot water
3 tablespoons orange juice
⅔ cup heavy cream
3 egg whites

Put the sugar in a saucepan with the water and heat gently until the sugar has dissolved, stirring. Add the fruit and cook gently for a few minutes until the juice is starting to run out. Purée and allow to become quite cold.

Place the gelatin in a small bowl with the cold water and leave for 3 minutes. Add the orange juice. Stand the bowl in a pan of simmering water and allow the gelatin to dissolve, cool slightly and stir into the fruit purée, leave until almost set.

Whisk the cream until it forms soft peaks and stiffly whisk the egg whites. Stir the cream into the purée and fold in the egg whites. Turn into a strong, glass mold or ovenproof dish.

To freeze: cover with a lid of foil, label and freeze.

To serve: thaw overnight in the refrigerator. If liked, the mousse may be decorated with a little whipped cream and fresh redcurrants before serving.

Pears in fresh raspberry sauce

¾ cup sugar
2½ cups water
6 pears
½ lb raspberries

Cooking Time: about 25 minutes

Put the sugar and water in a shallow pan and bring slowly to the boil, stirring, until all the sugar has dissolved. Cut the pears in half lengthwise, peel and with a teaspoon carefully scoop out the centers. Lay in the pan and gently poach for about 15 minutes or until tender; this will very much depend on the variety of pears used. Remove the pears and lay in a rigid container. Purée the raspberries and stir in enough of the sugar syrup to make a coating consistency, spoon over the pears.

To freeze: cover, label and freeze.

To serve: thaw overnight in the refrigerator, carefully spoon the pears into a serving dish and serve with plenty of whipped cream.
Serves 6

Easy lemon mousse

4 eggs
½ cup sugar
2 large lemons
⅓ oz gelatin
3 tablespoons water

Separate the eggs, place the yolks in a bowl with the sugar and beat until creamy. Grate the lemon rind finely, squeeze the juice from both lemons and add to the egg mixture. Put the gelatin in a small bowl or cup with cold water and leave to stand for 3 minutes. Stand the bowl in a pan of simmering water and allow the gelatin to dissolve. Cool slightly and stir into the lemon mixture, leave for a few minutes until the mixture starts to set. Whisk the egg whites until stiff and fold into the lemon mixture. Put into a straight-sided, strong glass mold or ovenproof dish.

To freeze: cover with a lid of foil, label and freeze.

To serve: remove the foil and thaw overnight in the refrigerator or for 4 hours at room temperature.

Strawberry fool; Redcurrant and raspberry mousse; Easy lemon mousse; Pears in fresh raspberry sauce

Strawberry fool

½ lb strawberries, hulled
1¼ cups heavy cream
¼ cup sugar
2 tablespoons Cointreau

Purée the strawberries. Whisk the cream until thick and fold in the sugar, strawberry purée and Cointreau. Turn into four strong individual serving pots.
To freeze: cover, label and freeze.
To serve: thaw in the refrigerator for 2 to 3 hours, decorate each fool with a halved strawberry and serve with Tuiles Almond Cookies (see page 83).

Bramble mousse

1 lb blackberries
½ cup sugar
2 tablespoons lemon juice
3 tablespoons cold water
⅓ oz gelatin
⅔ cup heavy cream
3 egg whites

Cooking Time: 8 minutes.

Pick over the blackberries and place in a saucepan, with the sugar and lemon juice, over a low heat, to draw the juices and dissolve the sugar, then cover and simmer gently for about 5 minutes, or until the fruit is soft.

Place the cold water in a bowl, sprinkle on the gelatin and leave to stand for 3 minutes. Draw the pan from the heat and add the gelatin, stir until dissolved.

Pass the fruit and juice through a strainer to make a purée, set aside until it is cold and shows signs of setting. Whisk the cream until it forms soft peaks, stiffly whisk the egg whites, fold both into the purée until evenly blended.

To freeze: turn into a strong, glass mold or ovenproof dish. Cover, label and freeze.

To serve: remove the cover and thaw overnight in the refrigerator, or 4 to 6 hours at room temperature. If liked, spoon into glasses, top each with a blackberry and serve with extra cream.

Fresh fruit salad

½ cup sugar
8 tablespoons water
1 tablespoon lemon juice
½ lb large black grapes, peeled and
pits removed
½ lb eating apples, peeled, cored and
sliced (about 1½ cups)
1 large orange, peeled and segmented
1 grapefruit, peeled and segmented
1 small honeydew melon, peeled, seeded
and cut in cubes
1 Charentais melon or cantaloup,
peeled, seeded and cut in cubes

Buy a quantity of fruit at a local market if you have one, if not buy when prices are reasonable. Do not buy over-ripe fruits as the freezer softens the texture slightly.

Dissolve the sugar in the water over a low heat. Cool, then stir in the lemon juice. Pour into a rigid container, stir in the fruit and mix well.

To freeze: cover, label and freeze.

To serve: thaw overnight in the refrigerator. If liked, add more fruit, eg fresh strawberries or cherries, bananas and pears, and stir in 2 tablespoons of orange liqueur.

Serves 8

Bramble mousse; Fresh fruit salad

Easy lemon cheesecake

⅓ lb graham crackers (1 pack)
4 tablespoons butter
3 tablespoons brown sugar
1 cup cream cheese
⅔ cup heavy cream
Small can condensed milk
¼ cup lemon juice

Crush the graham crackers with a rolling pin. Melt the butter in a pan, add the sugar then blend in the cracker crumbs and mix well, turn into a deep pie plate or flan dish and press into shape around the base and sides of the plate with the back of a spoon.
Place the cream cheese in a bowl, cream until soft and beat in the cream and condensed milk. Slowly add the lemon juice. Pour the mixture into the flan case.
To freeze: cover, label and freeze.
To serve: thaw overnight in the refrigerator. Garnish with a twist of lemon.

Sharp grapefruit cheesecake

⅓ oz gelatin
3 tablespoons cold water
2 8 oz packages cream cheese
6 oz can concentrated unsweetened grapefruit juice, thawed
Scant ½ cup sugar
1¼ cups heavy cream
¼ lb graham crackers
4 tablespoons butter
3 tablespoons brown sugar

Place the gelatin in a small bowl with the cold water and leave to stand for 5 minutes, then place in a pan of simmering water and leave to dissolve until the gelatin has become clear, remove and leave to cool. Cream the cheese until soft and gradually beat in the grapefruit juice and sugar. Stir in the cooled gelatin. Whisk the cream until thick but not stiff and fold into the cheesecake mixture. Turn into a lightly oiled 8 inch cake pan and place in the refrigerator. Crush the graham crackers finely. Melt the butter in a pan and stir in the crumbs and brown sugar, press over the cheesecake.
To freeze: cover with a lid of foil, label and freeze.
To serve: thaw overnight in the refrigerator. Turn out and decorate the cheesecake with whipped cream, strawberries, raspberries or grapes.

Ginger orange ring

1¼ cups heavy cream
½ lb ginger cookies

Whisk the cream until thick and use half to sandwich together the cookies and shape into a circle. An easy way is to put them in a loose-bottomed cake pan lined with a piece of foil, with a jam jar in the center, sloping the cookies slightly to fit in a circle around the jar.
Cover with the remaining cream.
To freeze: open freeze, then slip the cookie circle off the base of the cake pan, wrap in a double thickness of foil, seal, label and return to the freezer.
To serve: remove the wrapping, slip onto a serving dish and thaw in the refrigerator for 6 to 8 hours. Fill the center with orange segments, which have been mixed with superfine sugar and left to stand for at least an hour before using.

Sharp grapefruit cheesecake; Easy lemon cheesecake; Ginger orange ring

Raspberry pavlova

3 large egg whites
¾ cup superfine sugar
½ teaspoon white vinegar
2 teaspoons cornstarch

Cooking Time: 1 hour
Oven: 275°F

Whisk the egg whites until stiff, whisk in the sugar a spoonful at a time. Blend the vinegar with the cornstarch and whisk into the egg whites with the last spoonful of sugar.
Lay a sheet of baking paper on a baking sheet and mark an 8 inch circle on it. Spread the meringue out to cover the circle, building up the sides to come higher than the center.
Bake in the oven for 1 hour, then turn off the oven and leave the meringue until quite cold.
To freeze: place in a rigid container, cover, label and freeze.
To serve: place the meringue on a serving dish. Whisk 1¼ cups heavy cream until thick. Crush ½ lb of raspberries to a purée and stir into the cream, pile into the center of the meringue and decorate with ½ lb whole fresh raspberries. Leave to stand for an hour in the refrigerator before serving.
Serves 6 to 8

Hazelnut meringue gâteau

¼ lb hazelnuts
4 egg whites
1 cup superfine sugar
1 teaspoon white vinegar
⅔ cup heavy cream
3 tablespoons butter
3 tablespoons cocoa
3 tablespoons milk
¾ cup confectioners' sugar

Cooking Time: 45 minutes
Oven: 375°F

Place the hazelnuts on a tray and put into a moderately hot oven for a few minutes, tip onto a clean tea towel, rub them together well and the skins will flake off. Place in a blender and grind. Lightly brush the sides of two 8 inch layer cake pans with oil and line the base with non-stick parchment.
Whisk the egg whites until stiff, whisk in half the sugar a spoonful at a time, until the meringue is glossy. Mix the ground hazelnuts with the remaining sugar and fold into the meringue with the vinegar. Divide the mixture between the pans, spread flat and bake in the moderately hot oven for 45 minutes, then turn off the heat and leave to cool in the oven. Remove, turn out and peel off the paper. Whisk the cream until thick. Melt the butter in a small saucepan, stir in the cocoa and cook gently for 1 minute, stir in the milk and confectioners' sugar. Mix well to a thick spreading consistency and spread over one half of the meringue, spread the cream on the other half and sandwich together.
To freeze: open freeze, then pack in a large rigid plastic container, cover, label and return to the freezer.
To serve: place on a serving dish and thaw for at least 12 hours in the refrigerator. Dust with a little confectioners' sugar and decorate with chocolate flake before serving.
Serves 8

Ginger and pineapple meringue gâteau; Raspberry pavlova; Hazelnut meringue gâteau

Ginger and pineapple meringue gâteau

4 egg whites
½ cup superfine sugar
⅔ cup brown sugar
1¼ cups heavy cream
1 cup canned crushed pineapple, drained
2–3 pieces ginger, finely chopped

Cooking Time: 3–4 hours
Oven: 225°F

Line two large baking trays with non-stick baking paper or well greased wax paper. On one baking tray, mark out a circle 8 inches in diameter. On the other, mark one circle 7 inches and another 6 inches in diameter; use plates and saucers as guides. Whisk the egg whites with a whisk until they form peaks then add both the sugars in spoonfuls, whisking well after each addition. Divide the mixture between the marked circles and spread it out to cover.

Bake in a very cool oven for 3 to 4 hours, or until the meringues are firm to touch and dried out. Remove from the oven, leave to cool and peel off the paper. Whisk the cream until thick and fold in the pineapple and ginger. Spread half the cream on the largest piece of meringue, then cover with the next size of meringue, cover with the remaining cream and put the small meringue on top.

To freeze: open freeze, then pack in a large rigid plastic container (meringue is brittle when frozen), cover, label and return to freezer.

To serve: place on a serving dish and thaw in the refrigerator for at least 12 hours.

Serves 6 to 8

Chocolate simpkins; Chocolate and coffee torte; Special chocolate dessert cake

Chocolate simpkins

5 oz semi-sweet chocolate
2 eggs, separated
¼ cup sugar
⅔ cup heavy cream
½ cup glacé fruits, chopped
A little Cointreau to taste

Break the chocolate into small pieces, place in a bowl, stand over a pan of simmering water and leave until melted. Do not allow the chocolate to get too hot. Coat the insides of 6 small, strong molds or paper cupcake cases with the chocolate, using the handle of a teaspoon to make a smooth, even coating and leave to set.

Separate the eggs and whisk the yolks until well blended. Whisk the egg whites until stiff and whisk in the sugar a teaspoon at a time.

Whisk the cream until it holds soft peaks, then fold into the egg white mixture with the yolks, glacé fruits and Cointreau to taste.

Divide the mixture between the molds and smooth the tops.

To freeze: cover each mold with a piece of foil, seal, label, and freeze at once.

To serve: thaw at room temperature for about 5 minutes then gently ease out onto individual plates.

Serves 6

Special chocolate dessert cake

8 oz milk chocolate
½ lb margarine
2 eggs
2 tablespoons sugar
1 box imported Nice biscuits
Chocolate curls

This makes a special party dessert, because it looks so spectacular. Remove the ends from two 1 pound cans, wash and dry them thoroughly, then cover one end of each can with a double thickness of foil. Break the chocolate into small pieces, place in a pan with the margarine and heat gently until melted. Beat the eggs and sugar together until blended, then gradually add the chocolate mixture a little at a time. Break the biscuits into ½ inch pieces and blend into the chocolate mixture, pack into the two tins and leave in the refrigerator for 3 to 4 hours to set.

Remove the piece of foil from the base of each can, gently press out the chocolate rolls and push firmly together.

To freeze: wrap in a double thickness of foil, seal, label and freeze.

To serve: unwrap and place on a serving dish, cover with whipped cream and decorate with chocolate curls. Serve cut in slices.

Serves 8

Chocolate and coffee torte

6 tablespoons butter
½ cup sugar
Scant ⅓ cup cocoa
1 egg yolk
1 tablespoon sherry
¼ cup chopped hazelnuts
32 ladyfingers
¾ cup black coffee

Line an 8 inch round cake pan with foil. Cream the butter and sugar together until light and fluffy and then stir in the cocoa, egg yolk, sherry and nuts. Mix together well, adding a little extra sherry if necessary to make a spreading consistency.

Dip the ladyfingers, sugar side down, quickly in the coffee, arrange a layer in the bottom of the pan and cover with half the chocolate filling.

Put another layer of coffee-dipped ladyfingers on top, spread with the remaining filling, then cover with the rest, coffee side uppermost.

To freeze: cover with foil, seal, label and freeze.

To serve: thaw on a serving dish in the refrigerator for 3 to 4 hours. Cover with whipped cream, decorate with small meringues and chocolate curls and serve.

Serves 6 to 8

Plain scones

1¾ cups self-rising flour
1 teaspoon baking powder
¼ teaspoon salt
4 tablespoons margarine
About ⅔ cup milk to mix

Cooking Time: 8–10 minutes
Oven: 450°F

Sift the flour, baking powder and salt into a bowl. Rub in the margarine until the mixture resembles fine breadcrumbs. Make a well in the center and stir in sufficient milk to make a soft dough. Turn onto a floured table and knead until smooth, then roll out to about ¾ inch thickness. Cut into 8 rounds with a 2 inch cutter. Place on a greased baking sheet, brush with a little milk and bake at the top of a hot oven for 8 to 10 minutes, or until a pale brown. Cool on a wire rack.

To freeze: pack in a plastic bag, seal, label and freeze.

To serve: for speed, take the scones straight from the freezer and reheat in a hot oven for 10 minutes. If preferred, thaw at room temperature for 2 hours.

Makes 8 scones

Cheese scones

1¾ cups self-rising flour
¼ teaspoon salt
3 tablespoons margarine
½ cup grated Cheddar cheese
¼ cup grated Parmesan cheese
1 teaspoon dry mustard
About ⅔ cup milk to mix

Cooking Time: 10 minutes
Oven: 450°F

Sift the flour and salt into a bowl and rub in the margarine until the mixture resembles breadcrumbs. Mix the cheeses together and stir ½ cup into the bowl with the mustard. Add enough milk to make a soft dough. Turn onto a floured surface, knead lightly, then roll out to ¾ inch thickness. Cut into 10 rounds with a 2 inch cutter. Place on a greased baking sheet and sprinkle with the remaining cheese. Bake in a hot oven for 10 minutes, or until brown. Cool on a wire rack.

To freeze: pack in a plastic bag, seal, label and freeze.

To serve: as Plain Scones.

Makes 10 scones

Wholewheat scones

¾ cup wholewheat flour
¾ cup self-rising flour
2 teaspoons baking powder
¼ teaspoon salt
4 tablespoons margarine
About ⅔ cup milk

Make, bake, freeze and serve as Plain Scones.

Plain scones; Cheese scones; Wholewheat scones

70

Scotch pancakes

Lard for greasing
¾ cup self-rising flour
2 tablespoons sugar
1 egg
⅔ cup milk

Cooking Time: 10 minutes

Prepare a heavy frying pan, or electric frying pan, by rubbing the surface with salt and then greasing lightly with lard. When ready to cook the pancakes, heat the frying pan until the lard is just hazy, then wipe off any fat with paper towels.

Put the flour and sugar in a bowl, add the egg and half the milk and beat until smooth, then beat in the remaining milk. Spoon the mixture onto the heated surface in rounds, spacing well. When bubbles rise to the surface, turn the pancakes with a metal spatula and cook the .other side for ½ to 1 minute until golden brown. Place on a wire rack to cool while cooking the remaining mixture.

To freeze: when cold, place on a flat surface and open freeze. Stack neatly together and wrap in foil, seal, label and return to the freezer.

To serve: spread on a tray, put in a cold oven and turn the heat to 400°F for 10 to 15 minutes, or until warmed through. Serve while still warm, spread with butter.

Makes about 18 pancakes

Moist tacky gingerbread

1⅓ cups flour
2 teaspoons baking powder
2 teaspoons ground ginger
½ teaspoon ground allspice
Pinch of salt
4 tablespoons butter
⅓ cup brown sugar
1 tablespoon black treacle
1 tablespoon golden or light corn syrup
1 teaspoon baking soda
Scant cup warm milk
2 eggs, beaten
2–3 pieces ginger, finely chopped

Cooking Time: 40–50 minutes
Oven: 325°F

Grease an 8 inch square cake pan and line it with greased wax paper.

Sift the flour, baking powder, spices and salt into a bowl. Cream the butter with the sugar and treacle and syrup and beat well. Dissolve the baking soda in the milk and stir into the creamed mixture with the flour, beaten eggs and ginger. Beat well and pour into the pan. Bake in a warm oven for 40 to 50 minutes until well risen. Leave to cool in the pan.

To freeze: remove from the cake pan, wrap in foil, seal, label and freeze.

To serve: unwrap and leave to thaw at room temperature for 3 to 4 hours. If liked, this cake could be iced with a lemon icing.

Scotch pancakes; Moist tacky gingerbread; Homemade brown bread

Homemade brown bread

2 cups hand-hot water
1 teaspoon sugar
½ oz dry active yeast

Dough:
2⅔ cups all-purpose flour
2⅔ cups wholewheat flour
2 teaspoons sugar
1 tablespoon vegetable oil
Milk to glaze
A little cracked wheat

Cooking Time: 30–40 minutes
Oven: 450°F

Make the yeast liquid by mixing the water and sugar and stirring in the dried yeast. Leave for 10 to 15 minutes until frothy.
Put all the dry ingredients in a bowl. Pour on the yeast mixture and the oil and mix with a fork, then knead until smooth and no longer sticky, about 10 minutes. Grease a plastic bag with half a teaspoon of vegetable oil, put in the dough and leave to rise in a warm place, until doubled in bulk; this will take about an hour at room temperature. Knead until it returns to its original bulk. Shape it and put it in a greased 2 pound loaf tin. Glaze with milk and sprinkle with a little cracked wheat, cover with an oiled bag and leave to rise in a warm place until the dough has reached the top of the tin.
Remove the bag and bake in a hot oven for 30 to 40 minutes, or until the loaf is evenly browned and sounds hollow when tapped on the bottom.
To freeze: remove from tin, cool, wrap in a double thickness of foil or in a plastic bag, seal, label and freeze.
To serve: thaw for 3 to 4 hours at room temperature or overnight in the refrigerator.

Orange fruit teabread

Date and walnut cake

1¼ cups boiling water
½ lb dates, chopped
1 teaspoon baking soda
1 cup sugar
6 tablespoons butter
1 egg, beaten
Rounded 2 cups flour
1 teaspoon baking powder
½ teaspoon salt
⅓ cup chopped walnuts

For the Topping:
⅓ cup brown sugar
2 tablespoons butter
2 tablespoons milk
Walnut halves

Cooking Time: 1 hour
Oven: 350°F

Grease a 9 inch square cake pan and line it with greased wax paper. Put the water, dates and baking soda in a bowl and leave to stand for 5 minutes. Cream the sugar and butter together until soft then stir in the egg with the water and dates. Sift the flour with the baking powder and salt and fold in with the walnuts. Turn into the pan and smooth the top.
Bake in a moderate oven for 1 hour. Turn out and leave to cool on a wire rack.
Place all the topping ingredients, except the walnuts, in a pan and boil for 3 minutes, then spread over the cake. Decorate with walnut halves, and leave to set.
To freeze: wrap in a double thickness of foil, seal, label and freeze.
To serve: unwrap and thaw at room temperature for 5 to 6 hours.

Apricot fruit cake

1½ cups self-rising flour
Pinch of salt
¼ lb glacé cherries
16 oz can apricots
10 tablespoons butter
½ cup plus 2 tablespoons sugar
2 large eggs, beaten
2 tablespoons milk
¾ cup golden raisins
¾ cup dark raisins
¾ cup currants

Cooking Time: 2 hours
Oven: 325°F

Grease and line a 3 pound loaf tin with greased wax paper. Sift the salt and flour together. Halve the cherries, roll three-quarters of them in flour and keep the remainder for topping. Drain the apricots and chop finely. Cream the butter and sugar until light and creamy. Beat in the eggs, adding a tablespoon of flour with the last amount of egg. Fold in the flour, milk and all the fruit, except the cherries for the topping. Turn into the prepared tin and arrange the cherries on the top. Bake in a warm oven for 2 hours, or until cooked. Leave to cool in the tin.
To freeze: remove the paper and wrap in a double thickness of foil, seal, label and freeze.
To serve: unwrap and thaw at room temperature for about 6 hours.
Note: this is a very moist fruit cake and should be kept in the fridge wrapped in foil rather than in a cake tin.

Orange fruit teabread

Scant cup currants
Scant cup golden raisins
Scant cup brown sugar
Finely grated rind of 2 oranges
1¼ cups hot tea
Generous 2 cups self-rising flour
1 egg

Cooking Time: 1½ hours
Oven: 300°F

Put the fruit, sugar and orange rind in a bowl, pour over the hot tea, stir well, cover and leave to stand overnight. Grease and line with greased wax paper an 8 inch round cake pan. Stir the flour and egg into the fruit mixture and mix thoroughly.

Turn the mixture into the pan and bake in a cool oven for 1½ hours. Leave to cool on a wire rack.

To freeze: wrap in a double thickness of foil, seal, label and freeze.

To serve: thaw at room temperature for 4 to 5 hours and serve either sliced with butter or just as it is.

Date and walnut cake; Apricot fruit cake

Simnel cake

12 tablespoons (1½ sticks) butter, softened
1 cup brown sugar
3 eggs
1⅓ cups flour
3 teaspoons ground allspice
1 teaspoon baking powder
2 tablespoons milk
2 cups mixed dried fruit (golden raisins,
dark raisins and currants)
¼ cup glacé cherries, chopped
2 tablespoons mixed cut peel, chopped
Finely grated rind of 1 lemon
¼ cup ground almonds

Decoration:
1 lb almond paste
1 tablespoon sieved apricot jam
1 egg white
Foil-wrapped Easter eggs

Cooking Time: 2½ hours
Oven: 300°F, then increase to 425°F

Grease a round 7 inch cake pan and line it with greased wax paper. Put all the cake ingredients together in a large mixing bowl and beat together with a wooden spoon until well blended—this will take 2 to 3 minutes. Place half the mixture in the pan and smooth the top. Roll one-third of the almond paste to fit the pan and place on top of the cake mixture. Put the remaining mixture in pan and smooth the top.

Bake in a cool oven for 2½ hours, or until cooked, then leave to cool on a wire rack. Brush the top of the cake with the apricot jam. Roll out one-third of the remaining almond paste to a 7 inch round and place on the cake, pinching the edges. Roll out the remaining paste, shape into 11 balls and arrange them around the edge of the cake. If liked, brush with a little beaten egg white and bake at 425°F for 2 to 3 minutes to brown the almond paste lightly. Cool and decorate with Easter eggs.

To freeze: open freeze, then put in a large foil container, cover, label and freeze.

To serve: thaw at room temperature for 6 to 8 hours.

Christmas cake

2 cups flour
¼ teaspoon salt
1 teaspoon ground allspice
½ lb (2 sticks) butter
1⅓ cups brown sugar
1 tablespoon black treacle
4 eggs
2 lb mixed dried fruit (golden raisins,
dark raisins and currants)
¼ lb glacé cherries, quartered
¼ lb candied mixed peel, chopped
¼ cup almonds, blanched and chopped
2 tablespoons brandy

Cooking Time: 4 hours
Oven: 300°F, then reduce to 250°F

Line an 8 inch cake pan with a double thickness of greased wax paper. Sift together the flour, salt and spice. Cream the butter and sugar until light and beat in the treacle. Add the eggs one at a time, beating well after each addition and adding a spoonful of flour with each egg. Fold in the remaining flour. Add the dried fruit, cherries, peel and almonds and mix well. Place in the pan and make a hollow in the center.

Bake the cake in a cool oven for 3 hours, then reduce the oven temperature and bake for another hour, or until cooked. Cover the cake with a piece of brown paper if it is becoming too brown. Leave to cool in the pan for 20 minutes, then turn out, pierce with a skewer and spoon the brandy over the top and leave to cool.

To freeze: wrap in double thickness foil, seal, label and freeze.

To serve: thaw at room temperature for 6 to 8 hours.

Note: rich fruit cake improves with freezing. Thaw and ice this cake a week or so before Christmas.

Simnel cake; Christmas cake

Devil's food cake

Devil's food cake

$\frac{3}{4}$ *cup flour*
1 tablespoon cocoa
$\frac{1}{2}$ *teaspoon baking soda*
$\frac{1}{2}$ *teaspoon baking powder*
$\frac{1}{4}$ *cup sugar*
1 tablespoon golden or light
corn syrup
1 egg, beaten
6 tablespoons salad or corn oil
6 tablespoons milk

Cooking Time: 30–35 minutes
Oven: 325°F

Grease two 7 inch layer cake pans and line with greased wax paper. Sift the flour, cocoa, baking soda and baking powder into a mixing bowl. Make a well in the center and add the sugar and syrup. Gradually stir in the egg, oil and milk and beat well to make a smooth batter.

Pour into the pans and bake in a warm oven for 30 to 35 minutes, or until the tops spring back when lightly pressed with a finger.

Turn out and leave to cool on a wire rack. Sandwich together with Freezer Frosting (see page 86) and spread the remainder over the top and sides.

To freeze: open freeze, then place in a plastic bag, seal, label and return to the freezer.

To serve: remove the bag, place the cake on a plate and thaw at room temperature for about $4\frac{1}{2}$ hours.

Chocolate fudge cake

Chocolate fudge cake

4 oz semi-sweet chocolate
1¼ cups milk
⅔ cup brown sugar
1 teaspoon baking soda
¼ lb (1 stick) butter
¾ cup sugar
2 eggs, separated
1¾ cups flour, sifted

Icing:
9 tablespoons butter
9 tablespoons cocoa, sifted
2½ cups confectioners' sugar, sifted
Scant ⅔ cup milk

Cooking Time: 45 minutes
Oven: 350°F

Grease two 8 inch layer cake pans and line them with greased wax paper. Melt the chocolate in a saucepan with the milk and brown sugar until dissolved, but do not allow it to boil. Remove from the heat, add the baking soda and leave to cool. In a separate bowl, cream the butter with the sugar and beat in the egg yolks. Whisk the egg whites until stiff. Add by degrees the chocolate mixture and the flour to the creamed mixture, and lastly fold in the egg whites. Turn into the pans and bake in a moderate oven for 45 minutes, turn out and leave to cool. To make the icing, melt the butter in a small pan, stir in the cocoa and cook gently for 1 minute. Remove the pan from the heat, stir in the confectioners' sugar and sufficient milk to give a smooth, thick pouring consistency. Mix well and use to sandwich the cake together and pour the remaining icing over the cake.

To freeze: wrap in foil, seal, label and freeze.

To serve: thaw at room temperature for 5 to 6 hours. If liked, decorate with walnuts.

Basic Victoria layer cake

12 tablespoons (1½ sticks) butter
¾ cup sugar, warmed in the oven
3 eggs at room temperature
1⅓ cups self-rising flour

Cooking Time: 20–25 minutes
Oven: 375°F

This is one of the most useful standbys you can have in a freezer. It can take so many different fillings and toppings, can be eaten as cake or as part of another dessert, and makes a good partner for fruit. You can also vary the basic recipe by adding different flavorings.

Grease two 8 inch layer cake pans and line them with greased wax paper. Cream the butter and sugar together until light and fluffy. Beat the eggs and blend into the mixture, stirring in a spoonful of flour with the last egg. Sift in the remaining flour and turn into the two pans. Bake the cakes in a moderately hot oven for 20 to 25 minutes, or until the tops spring back when lightly pressed with the fingertips. Turn out onto a wire rack and cool.

To freeze: wrap in foil, seal, label and freeze.

To serve: thaw at room temperature for 4 to 5 hours, sandwich together with whipped cream and raspberry jam.

Variations on Victoria layer cake

Orange and lemon layer cake
Add the finely grated rind of 1 orange or lemon to the creamed mixture.

Chocolate layer cake
Replace 3 tablespoons flour with 3 tablespoons cocoa.

Coffee layer cake
Dissolve 1 heaping teaspoon instant coffee powder in the beaten eggs before adding to the mixture.

Cherry layer cake
Add ¼ cup halved glacé cherries to the mixture before adding in the flour.

Coconut layer cake
Add ⅓ cup dried coconut and 1 tablespoon milk with the flour.

Queen cakes
Add ½ cup dried mixed fruit (see page 76) and a few drops vanilla extract, and bake in muffin tins or cupcake cases for 15 to 20 minutes.

Butterfly cakes
Bake in muffin tins or cupcake cases. Cut a slice from the top of each cake and cut in half, spoon or pipe a little butter cream into the center of each cake, place the cake wings in the butter icing and dust with a little confectioners' sugar.

Coffee walnut layer cake
To a coffee cake mixture fold in ⅓ cup chopped walnuts with the flour and when cold fill and ice with coffee butter cream.

Note: all these flavors freeze well. The layer cake can be frozen filled with whipped cream or butter cream—but not with jam, as this tends to make the cake soggy.

Lemon sponge

Lemon sponge

3 eggs
Scant ½ cup sugar
⅔ cup self-rising flour
⅔ cup heavy cream
2 tablespoons lemon custard
or marmalade

Cooking Time: 20 minutes
Oven: 375°F

Grease two 7 inch layer cake pans and line them with greased wax paper. Put the eggs and sugar in a heatproof bowl over a pan of hot water and whisk until the mixture is thick, white and creamy and the whisk leaves a trail when lifted. Remove from the heat and whisk for another 2 minutes. Sift in the flour and carefully fold it in. Divide the mixture between the pans and bake in a moderately hot oven for 20 minutes, or until the tops spring back when lightly pressed with the fingertips. Turn onto a wire rack to cool. Whisk the cream until thick and blend in the lemon custard. Sandwich the cooled cakes with the lemon cream mixture.
To freeze: wrap in foil and a plastic bag, seal, label and freeze.
To serve: thaw overnight in the refrigerator or for 4 hours at room temperature, unwrap and sprinkle with sugar.

Tuiles almond cookies

Tuiles almond cookies

5 tablespoons butter
¼ cup sugar
4 tablespoons flour
¼ cup flaked almonds

Cooking Time: 8–10 minutes
Oven: 350°F

Cream the butter and sugar until pale and stir in the flour and almonds. Form into marble-sized balls and place half of them about 3 inches apart on a well greased baking sheet. Flatten with a damp fork and bake in a moderate oven for 8 to 10 minutes, until a pale golden brown.

Remove the baking sheet from the oven and leave for a few seconds then carefully lift the cookies off with a metal spatula, lay over a lightly oiled rolling pin and leave to harden. Repeat with the remaining mixture.

To freeze: pack carefully into a rigid container, cover, label and freeze.

To serve: thaw at room temperature for about an hour. Serve with mousses and fools.

Makes about 18

Note: these lose flavor quickly in a cake tin, but will keep if in the freezer.

Ginger spice cake

$\frac{1}{4}$ lb margarine
$\frac{1}{2}$ cup golden or light corn syrup
3 tablespoons black treacle
$\frac{2}{3}$ cup brown sugar
$\frac{2}{3}$ cup milk
2 eggs
$1\frac{3}{4}$ cups flour
2 teaspoons ground allspice
2 teaspoons ground ginger
1 teaspoon baking soda
1 cup golden raisins

Cooking Time: $\frac{3}{4}$ to 1 hour
Oven: 325°F

Grease an 8 inch square cake pan and line it with greased wax paper. Warm together the margarine, syrup, treacle and sugar, add the milk and allow to cool. Beat the eggs and blend with the cooled mixture. Sift the dry ingredients together, add the cooled mixture and the raisins, folding in with a spoon. Turn into the pan and bake in a warm oven for $\frac{3}{4}$ to 1 hour, or until well risen and golden brown. Turn out and leave to cool on a wire rack.
To freeze: wrap in foil, seal, label and freeze.
To serve: thaw at room temperature for 5 to 6 hours.

Freezer frosting

1 cup sugar
$\frac{2}{3}$ cup water
Pinch of cream of tartar
1 egg white, whisked

This is a good icing to use on cakes you are freezing. Put the sugar into a saucepan with the water and stir over a low heat until the sugar has dissolved. Bring to the boil and heat to 238°F, or until a small amount dropped in a saucer of cold water forms a ball. Remove from the heat, add the cream of tartar and beat lightly, until the syrup is just cloudy. Pour onto the stiffly whisked egg white, whisking all the time, and continue whisking until the mixture thickens and loses its shiny look. Use at once.

Ginger spice cake

Rich chocolate sauce

3 tablespoons butter
3 tablespoons cocoa, sifted
Small can evaporated milk
Scant cup confectioners' sugar, sifted

Melt the butter in a small saucepan, stir in the cocoa and cook for 1 minute. Remove from the heat, stir in the evaporated milk and confectioners' sugar and mix well.
To freeze: turn into a rigid plastic container, leave to cool, cover, label and freeze.
To serve: thaw at room temperature for 2 hours. Serve as a sauce with plain sponge cake, or over small choux pastry buns filled with whipped cream. It is also very good served over portions of ice cream.

Freezer frosting; Rich chocolate sauce

Chocolate fork cookies

½ lb (2 sticks) butter
½ cup sugar
1 teaspoon vanilla extract
1¾ cups self-rising flour
Rounded ⅓ cup cocoa mix
Confectioners' sugar and nuts (optional)

Cream the butter with the sugar and vanilla extract, then work in the flour and chocolate. Divide into pieces the size of a walnut and roll into balls, place on a baking sheet and flatten with a fork, dipped in cold water. Decorate with confectioners' sugar and nuts, if desired.

To freeze: open freeze, then pack into a rigid container, cover, label and freeze.

To cook: take straight from the freezer, place on a greased baking tray and bake in a moderately hot oven (375°F) for 12 to 15 minutes. Leave to firm for a minute on the baking tray, then cool on a wire rack.

Makes about 36 cookies

Chocolate crunch cookies; Brown sugar cookies

Chocolate fork cookies

Chocolate crunch cookies

1¾ cups flour
3 tablespoons cocoa
Pinch salt
12 tablespoons (1½ sticks) butter
½ cup superfine sugar
2 tablespoons granulated sugar

Cooking Time: 20 minutes
Oven: 325°F

Sift the flour and cocoa into a bowl with the salt. Cream the butter until soft, add the superfine sugar and beat until light and fluffy, then blend in the flour and work until smooth. Divide the mixture into two equal pieces each 6 inches long. Roll in the granulated sugar, then wrap in foil and chill in the refrigerator until firm. Grease two baking sheets, cut each roll into 16 slices, place on the baking sheets and bake in a warm oven for 20 minutes, or until the edges are turning a deeper shade of brown. Leave to cool on a wire rack.
To freeze: pack in a rigid container, cover, label and freeze.
To serve: remove from the container, thaw at room temperature for about 1 hour.
Makes 32 cookies

Brown sugar cookies

1¾ cups flour
Pinch salt
12 tablespoons (1½ sticks) butter
Scant cup brown sugar

Cooking Time: 20 minutes
Oven: 325°F

Sift the flour and salt into a bowl. Cream the butter until soft and then add three-quarters of the sugar and beat until light and fluffy. Blend in the flour and work until smooth. Divide the mixture into two equal pieces and roll out to form sausages each 6 inches long. Roll in the remaining sugar, then wrap in foil and chill in the refrigerator until firm. Grease two baking sheets, cut each sausage into 16 slices and place on the baking sheets. Bake in a warm oven for 20 minutes, or until the cookies are pale golden brown at the edges. Leave to cool on a wire rack.
To freeze: pack in a rigid container, cover, label and freeze.
To serve: remove from the container, thaw at room temperature for about 1 hour.
Makes 32 cookies

Coconut ice

3 cups sugar
1¼ cups water
2 pinches of cream of tartar
½ lb dried coconut
A little pink coloring

Cooking Time: about 20 minutes

Line a 7 inch square pan with wax paper. Dissolve half the sugar in half the water, add one pinch of cream of tartar, bring to the boil and boil to 238°F, or until a little of the syrup forms a soft ball when dropped into cold water. Remove from the heat and stir in half the coconut all at once. Pour into the prepared pan and leave to set.

Make a second quantity of coconut ice in the same way but, when adding the coconut, stir in a little pink coloring, avoiding over mixing. Spread over the first layer in the pan. When cold, cut in blocks and wrap in wax paper.

To freeze: overwrap in foil, seal, label and freeze.

To serve: thaw at room temperature for 5 to 6 hours.

Coconut ice

Raisin fudge

Small can evaporated milk
6 tablespoons butter
1 lb sugar (about 2¼ cups)
⅔ cup water
¼ teaspoon vanilla extract
½ cup golden raisins

Cooking Time: about 15 minutes

Butter a shallow 7 inch square pan. Put the evaporated milk, butter, sugar and water in a heavy pan, heat slowly until the sugar has dissolved, without boiling. Boil steadily to 237°F, stirring constantly, or until a small amount forms a soft ball when dropped into cold water. Remove from heat and add vanilla extract. Cool slightly and then beat, as the mixture thickens. Stir in the raisins as it starts to crystallize on the spoon.

Pour into the pan and leave to set. When firm, cut into 36 squares.

To freeze: pack in a rigid plastic container, cover, label and freeze.

To serve: remove from container, thaw in a single layer at room temperature for 1 to 2 hours.

Note: fudge makes a good Christmas present to give by hand—postage is out of the question as it is heavy stuff! Make ahead and freeze and it will certainly save time.

Raisin fudge

Easy Seville orange marmalade

Easy Seville orange marmalade

3 lb frozen Seville or other bitter oranges
7½ cups water
¼ cup lemon juice
6 lb (13–14 cups) sugar, warmed

Cooking Time: about 40 minutes

This marmalade is made from whole fruit in a pressure cooker and is an ideal way to use frozen Seville oranges. If you haven't a large pressure cooker, make half the quantity. The time to freeze oranges is between December and February—freeze them whole and use them for marmalade before the next season comes round. Put frozen oranges (do not thaw) and the water in the pressure cooker, cover and bring to 15 lb pressure for 20 minutes. Cool the pan in water to release the lid. Test the oranges for tenderness by pricking the skin with a pin. If it goes in easily the oranges are ready. Lift all the fruit out into a colander (catch any juice in a bowl underneath and return to the pan). Cut the oranges in half, remove all the pits and put the pits back into the pan, cover and bring to 15 pound pressure for another 5 minutes.
Meanwhile, slice all the orange peel shells, using a knife and fork on a wooden board, put this peel, lemon juice and warmed sugar in a large preserving pan, strain in water and juice from the pressure cooker and throw away the pits, stir over the heat to dissolve the sugar, then boil rapidly. Test for setting after 10 minutes. To do this, spoon a small amount onto a cold saucer—when it is cool, the skin that forms should wrinkle when pushed with the finger. Pour into hot clean jars, cover and label.
Makes 10 pounds marmalade.

Freezer mincemeat

Freezer mincemeat

1½ lb (about 5 cups) seeded dark raisins
¼ lb mixed peel
2 lb cooking apples
¾ lb (2¼ cups) currants
½ lb (2¼ cups) golden raisins
1 cup shredded suet
½ teaspoon ground allspice
¼ cup lemon juice
Finely grated rind of 2 lemons
1½ lb (3⅓ cups) sugar
6 tablespoons rum, brandy or sherry

Finely chop or mince the raisins. Peel, core and chop or mince the apples. Place the raisins and apples in a large bowl with the other fruit, suet and spice. Add the lemon juice and rind, sugar, and rum, brandy or sherry. Mix thoroughly and leave to stand overnight.
To freeze: turn into a large rigid container or, if preferred, several small ones. Cover, label and freeze.
To serve: thaw in the refrigerator overnight and use as required.
Note: this mincemeat needs to be kept in the freezer. Because of its high proportion of apple, it will not keep for more than a month in the refrigerator.

Egg and chive sandwiches

3 large eggs
6 tablespoons milk
1 tablespoon butter
3 teaspoons mayonnaise
2 teaspoons chopped chives
Salt and freshly ground black pepper

Scramble the eggs with the milk in the butter. Leave to cool and stir in the mayonnaise and chives. Season well.

Cream cheese and shrimp sandwiches

1 cup cream cheese
⅓ cup chopped shrimps
Salt and freshly ground black pepper

Combine the cheese and shrimps. Season well.

Sardine and tomato sandwiches

6 oz sardines, drained
2 tomatoes
Salt and freshly ground black pepper

Blend the sardines with the chopped tomatoes, season well.

To freeze the sandwiches:
Pack in layers with pieces of wax or freezer paper in between. Wrap in foil.
To serve: thaw at room temperature in the foil wrapping for 4 hours.

Black bread

Yeast Mixture:
1 teaspoon sugar
1¼ cups hand hot water
1 oz dry active yeast

Dough:
2⅔ cups rye flour
2⅔ cups all-purpose flour
1 teaspoon salt
1 tablespoon black treacle
⅔ cup milk
½ teaspoon caraway seeds
½ teaspoon vegetable oil

Cooking Time: 35–40 minutes
Oven: 425°F

To make up the yeast mixture, add sugar to water, sprinkle yeast on top. Stir well, leave 10–15 minutes, until frothy. To make up the dough, sift the flours and salt into a bowl. Add the treacle to the milk and warm slightly, then add the caraway seeds to the flour, make a well in the center and add the milk and treacle and the yeast mixture. Mix to a firm dough, put on a board, knead about 10 minutes.
Put into a plastic bag greased with ½ teaspoon vegetable oil and leave in a warm place until doubled in bulk, this will take about 1 hour at room temperature. Knead back to original bulk; this is called knocking back.
Divide the dough into 2 pieces and mold into 2 long loaves. Place on a well greased baking sheet, cover with oiled bags and leave to rise for about 40 minutes. Remove bags, brush with milk and bake for 35–40 minutes until browned and hollow sounding when tapped on base. Cool.
To freeze: wrap in a double thickness of foil or in a plastic bag, seal, label and freeze.
To serve: thaw at room temperature for 3 to 4 hours.

Sandwiches for the freezer: Egg and chive; Cream cheese and shrimp; Sardine and tomato. Black bread

Lemon sausage thyme stuffing

2 tablespoons butter
2 onions, peeled and finely chopped
1 lb pork sausage meat
3½ cups fresh white breadcrumbs
2–3 tablespoons finely chopped parsley
1 teaspoon fresh thyme, preferably lemon
thyme, or ½ teaspoon dried thyme
Finely grated rind of 1 lemon
2 tablespoons lemon juice
1 teaspoon salt
Freshly ground black pepper
1 egg, beaten

Cooking Time: about 10 minutes

Melt the butter in a pan, add the onion and fry until soft, about 10 minutes. Stir in the remaining ingredients and mix well together.
To freeze: put in a plastic bag, seal, label and freeze.
To serve: thaw in the refrigerator overnight, then use to stuff a turkey.
Makes enough to stuff a 12 pound turkey.
Note: fresh herbs give this stuffing a much better flavor than dried ones.

Croûtons

Cut slices of white bread, remove the crusts and cut into ½ inch cubes. Fry in shallow or deep fat until crisp and golden. Drain thoroughly on paper towels.
To freeze: pack in plastic bags, seal, label and freeze.
To serve: place uncovered, but still frozen, in a moderately hot oven (400°F) for about 5 minutes.

Mint sauce

Large bunch of mint, finely chopped
1 cup sugar
1¼ cups water

Divide the mint among the sections of an ice-cube tray. Place the sugar and water in a saucepan and heat gently until the sugar has dissolved, then boil gently for 3 to 4 minutes. Pour over the mint in the ice tray. Cool.
To freeze: open freeze until solid, then remove cubes from tray and put in a plastic bag, seal, label and return to freezer.
To serve: thaw the number of cubes required in a sauce boat and add a little vinegar to taste.

Brandy butter

12 tablespoons (1½ sticks)
unsalted butter
2⅔ cups confectioners' sugar, sifted
4–6 tablespoons brandy

Cream the butter with a wooden spoon until it is soft. Gradually beat in the confectioners' sugar and continue beating until the mixture is light and soft. Beat in the brandy.
To freeze: turn into a small rigid container, cover, label and freeze.
To serve: thaw for 12 hours at room temperature, turn into a small serving dish.

Chestnut stuffing; Brandy butter; Croûtons; Lemon sausage thyme stuffing; Mint sauce

Chestnut stuffing

15½ oz can whole chestnuts in water,
drained and chopped
1¾ cups fresh wholewheat breadcrumbs
Finely grated rind of ½ lemon
1 large egg, beaten
4 tablespoons butter
1 onion, peeled and chopped
Salt and freshly ground black pepper

Cooking Time: about 10 minutes

Place the chestnuts in a bowl with the breadcrumbs, lemon rind
and beaten egg. Melt the butter in a small pan, add the onion and
cook gently for about 10 minutes or until soft. Add to the bowl with
the seasoning and mix well.
To freeze: turn into a plastic bag, seal, label and freeze.
To serve: thaw in the refrigerator overnight and then use to stuff
a turkey.
Makes enough for a 12 pound turkey.

Index